Tales from the
Whispering Woods

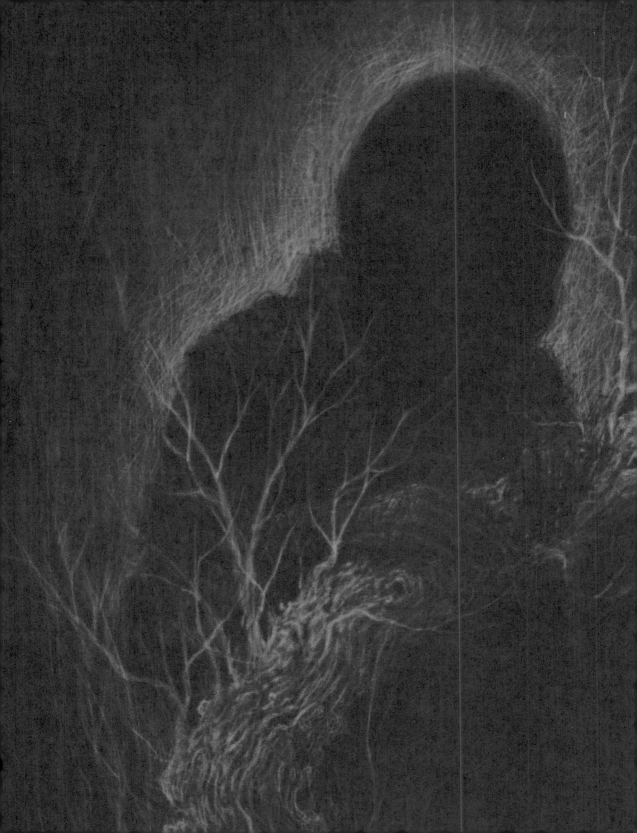

Tales from the
Whispering Woods

STORIES OF FEAR AND FOLKLORE
FROM THE DARK FOREST

Sarah J H Powell

castle

TO MY FAMILY AND LISTENERS OF
THE WHISPERING WOODS PODCAST.

Contents

Introduction

The woods have always whispered their secrets through the gnarly old branches of thousand-year-old oaks. They murmur them through the clearings where the bracken swells and bends to its familiar song. At first, this dance is full of energy, but it swiftly changes to a danse macabre, reminding us of the universality of life. The words are whispered through the grassy meadows and the sacred trees of these lands: the Oak, ʻŌhiʻa Lehua, Hawthorn, Palo Santo, and Baobab, to name but a few. They whisper through the ancient landscapes, the holloways, and megaliths—but you must listen closely, or you won't hear your ancestors' secrets, warnings, and stories. Do you long to listen to their tales, full of mystery, intrigue, and terror?

As you stand at the edge of the wildwood, the whispers grow more intense. It's a siren's call that will not be silenced, and your steps begin to falter. The air is thick with the scent of moss and decay, a fragrance that speaks loudly of the cycle of life and death. The forest floor is soft beneath your feet, a carpet of fallen leaves and ancient soil that has known the tread of countless beings.

The trees are ancient watchers, their bark gnawed by the passage of time, their leaves rustling with the secrets they guard. The deeper you venture, the more the forest comes alive, as if each step awakens long-slumbering spirits. Shadows flit between the trees, shapes, and figures that are gone when you turn to look.

The wind carries voices, fragments of ancient songs and long-lost languages that weave through the air like delicate silk threads, wisping in the breeze. They tell of battles fought and loves lost, the rise and fall of empires that have faded into myth. History breathes in the heart of the wildwood, as the past is never truly gone.

This book features tales from twenty-one trees of the wildwood that hail from every corner of the world, from the distant reaches of the past to the familiar shores of the present. These trees, viewed as culturally significant and, sometimes, even sacred among the people with whom they have coexisted peacefully for centuries, have much wisdom to impart. Indeed, in many cultures, trees are not merely silent spectators to the passing of time: They are active participants in the narrative of life.

Each tree has its own voice. It is the keeper of its peoples' stories. They are connected to one another by their roots and branches and the shared tales that have grown around them—tales of creatures and phenomena that they have been appointed to pass down in this book. The trees hold the secrets of these creatures' origins and purpose and, perhaps, even the reasons for their terrifying traits. But hold fast and don't run away, for though their words may frighten at first, you will also learn how to avoid falling victim to these chimeras yourself.

Furthermore, lest you remain a skeptic, each account ends with stories inspired by real-life encounters and events—cautionary tales of ordinary humans who encountered these horrifying nightmares in their waking lives.

The trees have long wanted to pass their stories down to those who will listen, for they, more than anyone or anything, know how swift and cruel the passage of time is to these delicate threads that we call stories. To tell these tales ensures their immortality—not only of the stories themselves but of the people, places, and cultures that created them.

Will you dare to embrace the wisdom they offer? Or will you flee, leaving unexplored the mysteries of the forest? The decision is yours, but know this: The wildwood has chosen you. Here, where the veil between worlds is so delicate, you may find answers to questions you never thought to ask and truths that will change you forever.

Let's begin our journey and wander into the dark forest. Put your best foot forward and take a deep breath. In this place of power, where the night reigns supreme, you will discover that you are part of a story much more significant than your own.

Welcome to the wildwood, where every whisper is a story, and every shadow hides a secret.

Tales of Black Dogs

THE HAWTHORN TREE

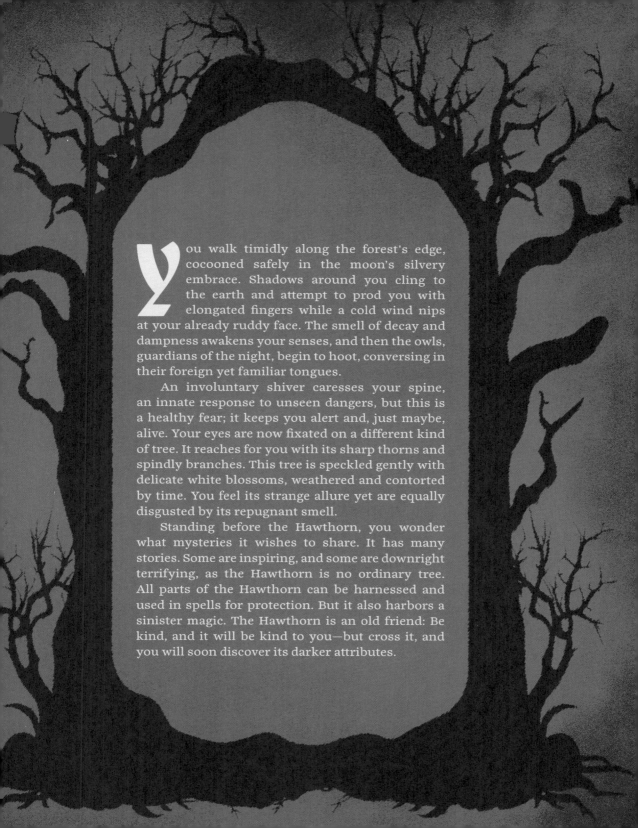

Y ou walk timidly along the forest's edge, cocooned safely in the moon's silvery embrace. Shadows around you cling to the earth and attempt to prod you with elongated fingers while a cold wind nips at your already ruddy face. The smell of decay and dampness awakens your senses, and then the owls, guardians of the night, begin to hoot, conversing in their foreign yet familiar tongues.

An involuntary shiver caresses your spine, an innate response to unseen dangers, but this is a healthy fear; it keeps you alert and, just maybe, alive. Your eyes are now fixated on a different kind of tree. It reaches for you with its sharp thorns and spindly branches. This tree is speckled gently with delicate white blossoms, weathered and contorted by time. You feel its strange allure yet are equally disgusted by its repugnant smell.

Standing before the Hawthorn, you wonder what mysteries it wishes to share. It has many stories. Some are inspiring, and some are downright terrifying, as the Hawthorn is no ordinary tree. All parts of the Hawthorn can be harnessed and used in spells for protection. But it also harbors a sinister magic. The Hawthorn is an old friend: Be kind, and it will be kind to you—but cross it, and you will soon discover its darker attributes.

As you nestle your back against the tree's rough bark, the Hawthorn leans in, its voice a gentle susurrus. "The Black Dogs," it whispers, "roam the shrouded moors and ancient crossroads of Britain. Across this land, the legends of Black Dogs descend through time, entangled with the peoples' constant dread of death. They are more than flesh and bone—not just canines, but also symbols and carriers of forgotten fears.

"The Black Dogs prowl this rugged terrain, seeking prey and spreading terror. These spectral hounds stalk the countryside during the darkest hours with eyes like burning coals. They are the wordless watchers, the guardians of thresholds, and omens of fate. With fur as dark as the night sky and a presence that will chill your soul, they are known by many names—Black Shuck, Padfoot, Barghest—each name carrying tales of mystery and despair.

"These Black Dogs are more than phantoms of folklore. They embody the land's ancient spirit. A spirit that careens through the core of British tales, reminding you that there are things beyond the realm of the living.

"Those who encounter these hounds often speak of a feeling of foreboding, a sense that the dog is a harbinger of doom or, in rarer cases, a protector against evil spirits. These encounters, whether real or imagined, have left a lasting impression on the psyche of the British people, shaping their beliefs and folklore.

"The physical forms of these spectral canines defy the ordinary. Some are headless, with necks ending in a jagged stump. Others possess two heads, their eyes glowing with an evil intensity. Their bodies ripple with unsettling energy as if they exist simultaneously in our world and Erebus, a manifestation of supernatural powers.

"The Black Dogs of British lore do not hunger for flesh; their appetite is for life itself. They stalk the edges of existence, where the shroud between worlds is, at best, flimsy. Their eyes, aglow with a terrifying light, pierce through the darkness, reflecting your inner demons and fears.

"As the Black Dogs glide silently over the land and their footfalls leave no trace, their passage is often marked by a sudden drop in temperature or an unexplained sense of unease. They are keepers of secrets and the bearers of messages from the beyond. To see a Black Dog is to be reminded of the mysteries that lurk just out of sight, in the corners of our world where the unknown still reigns.

"The true origins of the Black Dogs remain a mystery. Were they birthed from the cauldrons of Celtic lore or forged by the ancient Germanic pyres that once blazed across Britain? Like my gnarled roots, their lineage is a labyrinth of forgotten epochs.

Similar Creatures in Folklore

Moddey Dhoo
ISLE OF MAN

Both sinister and protective, the Moddey Dhoo is a phantom hound that roams ancient sites.

Old Shuck
EAST ANGLIA, ENGLAND

Old Shuck is a shadowy Black Dog, often seen on lonely roads and near graveyards.

Whisht Hounds/Yeth
DEVON, ENGLAND

The Whisht Hounds are part of English folklore, often associated with the Wild Hunt (page 106). They roam the moors and forests during the dark hours.

Gytrash or Guytrash
YORKSHIRE, ENGLAND

A shape-shifting Black Dog, sometimes appearing as a horse or other animal.

Galley Hill Black Dog
LUTON, BEDFORDSHIRE, ENGLAND

Associated with a storm that set a gibbet (an instrument of public execution) on fire in the sixteenth or seventeenth century.

Cù-Sìth/Cu Sidhe
SCOTLAND AND IRELAND

A ghostly green hound said to abduct nursing mothers, forcing them to nurse the fairy children.

Gwyllgi, Dog of Darkness
WALES

Described as a massive black wolf or mastiff with flaming eyes and foul breath.

"In Celtic myth and beyond, these canines assume a different guise—they become guardians of the Underworld, leading souls to the afterlife. The Welsh Ci Annwn has eyes like moonlit pools; the Norse Garmr is fierce and unyielding; and the Greek Cerberus is a three-headed keeper of Hades. These entities, with their unique traits and roles, may have sown the seeds for the later tales of the Black Dogs, with each culture imbuing them with their own symbolism and significance.

"Or perhaps they are the misinterpretation of encounters with perilous creatures—wolves, even giant dogs—that prowled the lonely bridleways. Moonlight caught in their eyes blazed like twin lanterns, setting them apart from ordinary wildlife. To the frightened observer, these were not mere beasts but otherworldly sentries whose gaze pierced through to the soul.

"So, my friend, as you wander the lonely paths of Britain under the moon's pale light, be mindful of the Black Dogs. They are the manifestation of the land's soul, the spectators of centuries of stories, and the carriers of the night's deepest secrets.

"Take heed, for I shall share wisdom as ancient as the roots that bind me to the soil. When darkness engulfs the land and solitude wraps you in a suffocating shroud, these protection rites against the Black Dogs are not just a precaution: They are your only salvation. Clasp iron close to your breast, for it is a potent talisman against evil. This metal will repel many malevolent monsters. Let it be your silent companion, a defense forged in earthly fires.

"When the Black Dogs materialize from the shadows, avoid their fiery gaze. Lower your eyes quickly, lest they penetrate your soul, for their eyes hold secrets and curses. To meet their stare is to invite peril. Seek sanctuary in hallowed places: a church, its timeworn stones steeped in prayer, or perhaps a crossroads, where paths intersect and destinies entwine. There, the shroud between our world and theirs thins, and the Black Dogs may hesitate. Remember, wanderer, these are not just superstitions. This advice may be your lifeline in the face of the hounds of hell.

"My new friend, you must heed my words, or not, at your peril. Black Dogs are not mere folklore. They represent the peoples' fears of the dark; they are the guardians and harbingers of fate."

The Watcher of the Shoreline

APRIL 1972, GORLESTON-ON-SEA, ENGLAND

In the spring of 1972, Coastguard George Abbott, a man of practicality and salt-encrusted boots, had recently been stationed at the Gorleston rescue headquarters. His arrival coincided with the shifting of tides as if fate itself had drawn him to this desolate stretch of coastline. Little did he know that the keening winds carried more than salt and sea spray.

They bore the burden of the beast.

On that fog-drenched morning, as dawn painted the sky in an incredible array of red-orange hues, George stood, observing at the cliff edge. His watchful eyes scanned the waters, where bulldozers had recently razed the dunes, leaving the beach empty and exposed.

And then, it materialized.

A hound that was blacker than the darkest night emerged from the horizon. Its form stood sharply against the muted expanse of the shoreline. The creature moved with a purpose that was both terrifying and fascinating as its sinewy muscles propelled it forward. It ran and then halted abruptly, tethered by invisible chains from which it could not break loose. The dog's eyes held him captive, fiery orbs in a sunless sky. George blinked his eyes rapidly. The supernatural nature of the hound was undeniable.

George's heart pounded as he watched. The spectral dog's gaze seemed to punch between worlds.

And then, as swiftly as it had arrived, the phantom hound vanished. George rubbed his eyes, but the beach remained empty: a void where the creature once stood, and all that was left was a sense of the uncanny.

Curiosity gnawed at him and he shared the strange sighting with his colleagues, the grizzled seafarers who knew the coast's secrets. "Have you ever seen anything like it?" he asked. His colleagues exchanged glances. "Aye, lad," one of them finally spoke, his voice a raspy, low rumble. "We've heard of the Gorleston beast, though we don't much speak of it. He's a watcher of the shoreline and a precursor to powerful storms."

"The locals call it Black Shuck," said Old Tom, his voice a gasp of the sea and shingled beaches.

Black Shuck. The name resonated and struck a chord deep within George. The scientist in him scoffed at such notions, but the part of him that had seen the canine's intense eyes couldn't help but wonder.

And so, Coastguard George Abbott became a seeker of shadows. As the crashing waves and howling winds whispered their archaic requiem, he stepped into the mist, following the footfalls of the spectral hound. The fog wrapped around him like a cloak, its tendrils cold and damp against his skin, its scent of salt and surf filling his nostrils.

And somewhere, in the heart of the shore, Black Shuck awaited—a terrifying beast with eyes alight, watching and waiting.

Legends of large black dogs continue to be sighted around Britain across various regions, from the rugged moors of Yorkshire to the mist-shrouded cliffs of Wales. Witnesses to this day share eerie accounts of encounters with these phantom canines, their eyes like blazing embers and their presence both captivating and unsettling.

Shadow of the Abbey: Unearthing the Legend of Black Shuck

Back in 2013, archaeologists from British social enterprise DigVentures found the bones of a giant dog buried in a shallow grave in the ruins of Leiston Abbey in Suffolk, England. The skeletal remains were estimated to be from a creature that would have once stood over seven feet (2 m) on its hind legs and weighed approximately two hundred pounds (91 kg). Scientists say the bones are possibly from the medieval period. Was this Black Shuck himself?

The Wendigo's Hunger

THE MANIDOO-GIIZHIKENS TREE

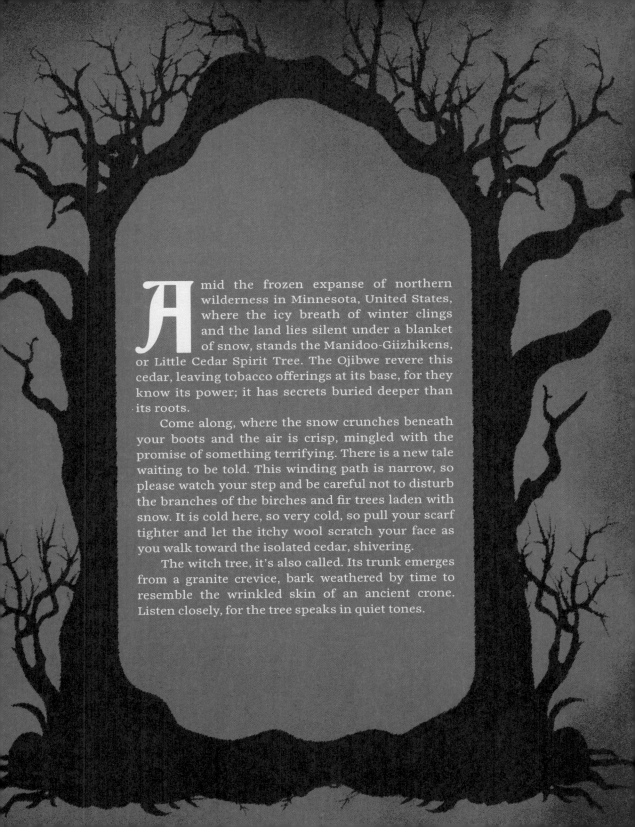

Amid the frozen expanse of northern wilderness in Minnesota, United States, where the icy breath of winter clings and the land lies silent under a blanket of snow, stands the Manidoo-Giizhikens, or Little Cedar Spirit Tree. The Ojibwe revere this cedar, leaving tobacco offerings at its base, for they know its power; it has secrets buried deeper than its roots.

Come along, where the snow crunches beneath your boots and the air is crisp, mingled with the promise of something terrifying. There is a new tale waiting to be told. This winding path is narrow, so please watch your step and be careful not to disturb the branches of the birches and fir trees laden with snow. It is cold here, so very cold, so pull your scarf tighter and let the itchy wool scratch your face as you walk toward the isolated cedar, shivering.

The witch tree, it's also called. Its trunk emerges from a granite crevice, bark weathered by time to resemble the wrinkled skin of an ancient crone. Listen closely, for the tree speaks in quiet tones.

You wiggle your back against the tree to make yourself comfortable. The Little Cedar delays briefly—it likes to tease, for such stories should never be rushed. "The Wendigo," it starts, "is beyond corporeal existence. It is an embodiment of the peoples' collective yearnings and terrors. It is a complex being which, born from hunger and desperation, teaches a lesson against greed and selfishness.

"The Wendigo soars high above the frosty pines during the cold and bitter months. With an emaciated face, it lacks lips and cheeks as it has chewed them off in desperation. The Wendigo is more than just a creature of the wild places. It reflects your own human darkness, a darkness that prioritizes your own survival above all others. Those who feast on their own kind risk becoming a receptacle for the Wendigo. Their hearts and spines, encased in ice, become carriers of this disease, unraveling communities where trust and cooperation are vital for survival. The cold and famine that grip the North American wastelands find embodiment in the Wendigo.

"The term 'Wendigo' comes from the Ojibwe word Wiindigoo. Yet it also appears in other Indigenous folklore with alternative translations and variations—for instance, the Cree refer to it as Wīhtikow and sometimes Wetiko. No matter the linguistic differences, this monster is always nefarious and cannibalistic. With a gaunt figure and desiccated skin stretched tightly over its bones, it is utterly terrifying. It can have skeletal horns, sunken eyes, and lips that are tattered and bloody.

"According to the legends, the Wendigo possesses the bodies of those who resort to cannibalism. It can never be satiated, for its size grows with every human it eats. It can also fly, become invisible, or possess humans, and it exudes a fetid stench of decay and corruption. In some myths, the Wendigo is perceived as a spirit rather than a physical being. In Cree mythology, it is considered a sinister force that inhabits people. The toxin enters a person by the bite of a Wendigo or through dreams. Once possessed, the affected individual may exhibit cannibalistic tendencies or other disturbing characteristics.

"The Wendigo is born from the harsh and unforgiving landscape. It symbolizes the struggle for survival, isolation, and the delicate balance between community and self. This story carries a cautionary message that is carried through the ages.

"When hope was gnawed by the hoar of those bone-chilling winters, a choice loomed: share or devour. The Wendigo, born from this desperate crossroads, embodies that fateful decision. Its transformation is a chilling metamorphosis, commencing with the gnawing ache of desire—a hunger not only for sustenance but also for power and possessions. It becomes a creature of gluttonous appetite, a symbol of the destructive power of unchecked greed and the consequences it can bring.

Similar Creatures in Folklore

Atshen

INNU

A cannibalistic spirit whose hunting grounds encompass the Innu peoples' traditional homeland on the east coast of modern-day Canada. These creatures are humans who have turned into insatiable beasts as a result of cannibalism.

Wechuge

NORTH AMERICAN ATHABASKAN

A man-eating creature believed to be a person possessed by the power of an ancient giant spirit animal. Like the Wendigo, one who suffers the curse of the wechuge becomes a destructive and cannibalistic creature that seeks to consume people. It can only be defeated by being thrown onto a campfire and kept there until it melts.

Ghoul

VARIOUS MYTHOLOGIES, INCLUDING ARABIC FOLKLORE

Ghouls are wicked spirits or phantoms that eat the flesh of the dead. They are emaciated, corpse-like beings with sharp claws and long limbs. They prowl at night, seeking cadavers to consume. In some legends, they can shape-shift into humans to deceive their victims. They're believed to haunt burial grounds, crypts, and dark corners.

"Take heed, wanderer. The Wendigo's icy breath chills more than flesh; it punctures the soul. It is the moral compass forged in the frost, urging you to share your meager firewood, your last morsel of food. Survival is not solitary. It thrives in the collective breath of kinship, in the warmth of shared resources and compassion. The Wendigo's presence is a constant reminder of the importance of communal responsibility—that your individual actions can either strengthen or weaken the tribe's resilience in the face of its hunger.

"When winter's grip tightens, the Wendigo emerges a spectral entity. Its eyes, like frigid sparks, scan the snow-kissed horizon. It is not just a nudge to the weary, but a call to action: Stand together. Seek refuge. The Wendigo is a reminder of the strength in unity and shared accountability.

"Now, dear wanderer, some believe that protective amulets or charms can ward off the Wendigo and fire can harm it, though its wounds heal swiftly. Legends are divided on the method of defeating the Wendigo: Some encourage cutting out its heart and burning it, while most agree that only a shaman can truly defeat and subdue this ancient wraith.

"Esteemed companion, heed my words at your discretion, yet know the peril of ignoring them. The Wendigo embodies voracity, metamorphosis, and the elemental powers that carve your fate."

The Call of the Wendigo

DECEMBER 2019, ONTARIO, CANADA

Marco, the protagonist of this tale, cannot tell you for sure what he heard on that cold December day. But the sky had filled with unease; something evil was coming. Marco perceived it keenly—a subtle gnawing at first, but as the day waned, it strengthened into a ravenous maw that tore down all his senses. They were deep in the heart of the wilderness, a place where survival was a constant battle.

Marco, his wife, and their young grandson had set off early for the grouse hunt near where they lived, in the heart of northwestern Ontario, Canada. The sun, at first a golden orb, now cast wraith-like shadows on the forest floor. The air darkened and thickened, and an impenetrable uneasiness had settled over the family—a feeling of being watched, of being prey.

Marco's boots crunched through the snow as he tried to make sense of this feeling, but it remained frustratingly elusive. His wife walked behind him with their young grandson; the boy's rosy cheeks peeked out through the gap between his hat and coat, eyes wide with wonder.

The pines creaked and moaned as Marco adjusted the shotgun on his shoulder, the metal chilly against his exposed, ruddy neck. A few steps farther and even the cackling grouse fell silent.

Then, as if hailed by archaic forces, a haunting sound stabbed through the stillness. It was a noise that defied the norm—a guttural howl reverberating with hunger. Marco's heart raced, his breath caught in his throat, and he exchanged glances with his wife. Her eyes were wide with terror, mirroring his own, reflecting their shared fear.

A realization that the hunter was now the hunted.

"What is that?" His wife asked, her voice barely a whisper.

Marco, who was a well-seasoned outdoorsman, quickly hushed his wife to strain his ears as she looked at him expectantly. This was not the calls of moose, wolves, or bears. It was something else—an unearthly cry that echoed through the trees. Each note drove a chill up his spine.

Mouth agape, Marco's trembling hands reached for his phone. Instinct drove him to record the anonymous din. "There's something not right about this," he murmured. "I've never heard anything like it."

Their young grandson was nestled against his wife, seemingly oblivious to his grandparents' horror. The child's innocent eyes widened as he absorbed the strange sounds. And then, the little one began to mimic the howls. His voice was sweet and pure in stark contrast to the haunting song.

"We should leave," Marco's wife urged. "This place is cursed." Her voice quivered with worry and concern as her eyes darted nervously around the darkening woodland.

But Marco hesitated; he needed answers. He needed proof. So, with trembling fingers, he raised his phone high and captured the vitriolic whines. The wails grew louder and closer.

Marco's wife clutched their grandson, her eyes wide with knowing. "I'm going," she whispered, rushing back to the car.

Marco followed but couldn't tear his eyes from the shadows. The Wendigo—for surely it was this creature of the wilderness—had singled him out. Its call resonated deep within.

As they retreated from the forest's heart, the howls followed. Back home, Marco uploaded his evidence to the internet—perhaps a desperate plea for validation. Biologists from Ontario's ministry weighed in, but their expertise faltered. No known creature matched these ungodly sounds.

The Wendigo Trials: A Tale of Shamanic Justice and Colonial Law

In 1907, two Ojibwe brothers, Jack and Joseph Fiddler, were arrested by the Canadian authorities and accused of murdering fourteen people. The brothers maintained that the victims were either Wendigo or in the process of becoming such creatures. Jack was a shaman and Wendigo hunter, and he was revered in his community for his knowledge and skills regarding these beasts. Despite their defense, both men were locked up for the killings, and Jack took his own life shortly after. The case of the Fiddler brothers is often cited as a poignant example of the clash between Indigenous practices and colonial legal systems that were imposed upon them.

The Nightmares of the Dab Tsog

THE BANYAN TREE

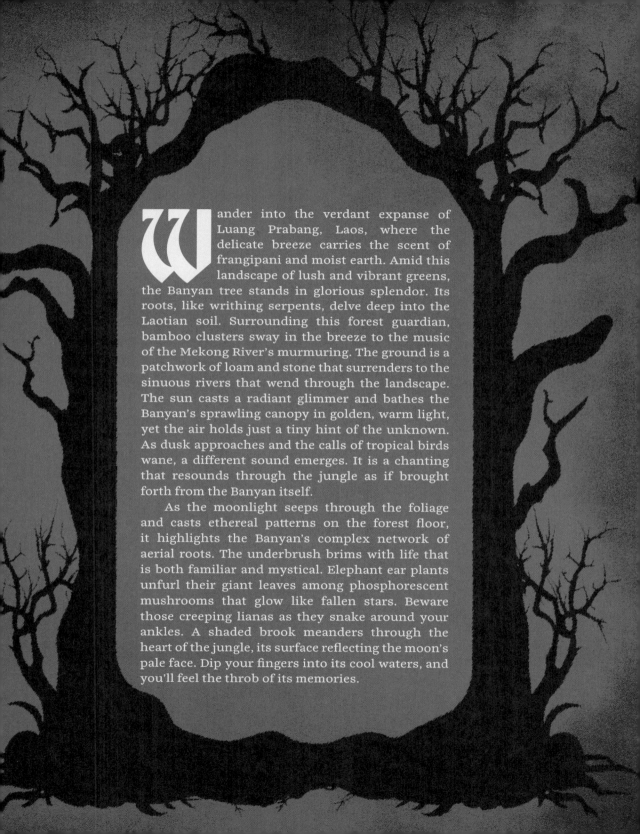

Wander into the verdant expanse of Luang Prabang, Laos, where the delicate breeze carries the scent of frangipani and moist earth. Amid this landscape of lush and vibrant greens, the Banyan tree stands in glorious splendor. Its roots, like writhing serpents, delve deep into the Laotian soil. Surrounding this forest guardian, bamboo clusters sway in the breeze to the music of the Mekong River's murmuring. The ground is a patchwork of loam and stone that surrenders to the sinuous rivers that wend through the landscape. The sun casts a radiant glimmer and bathes the Banyan's sprawling canopy in golden, warm light, yet the air holds just a tiny hint of the unknown. As dusk approaches and the calls of tropical birds wane, a different sound emerges. It is a chanting that resounds through the jungle as if brought forth from the Banyan itself.

As the moonlight seeps through the foliage and casts ethereal patterns on the forest floor, it highlights the Banyan's complex network of aerial roots. The underbrush brims with life that is both familiar and mystical. Elephant ear plants unfurl their giant leaves among phosphorescent mushrooms that glow like fallen stars. Beware those creeping lianas as they snake around your ankles. A shaded brook meanders through the heart of the jungle, its surface reflecting the moon's pale face. Dip your fingers into its cool waters, and you'll feel the throb of its memories.

You sit beside the Banyan tree and shift gently upon the cold and wet earth. A murmured complaint escapes your pursed lips as a rock digs into your backside. You nudge it deftly away. The ancient and wise Banyan releases a mournful sigh as it bewails your lost vision—lost to the mundane at the sake of the extraordinary. Its voice is as radiant as the moon's corona as it breaks the silence. "The Dab Tsog," the Banyan sings, "is not just a nightmare. It embodies your inner battles and the delicate equilibrium you crave.

"In the whispered lore of the Hmong people, there lurks a maleficent specter known as Dab Tsog or Dab Tsuam. It is a malevolent wraith that preys upon the sleeping. It is said to perch upon the chests of its victims, causing the sensation of being crushed or paralyzed and rendering the victim unable to move or speak. The Dab Tsog is a formless entity, though sometimes envisioned as a spiteful crone, a large dog, or a cat. It defies the confines of simple classification but is known to be one of the many 'pressing spirits' of folklore.

"Pressing spirits are not only a figment of lore but a manifestation of the primal dread that sleep paralysis evokes. This ghastly phenomenon inflicts itself upon unfortunate souls whose minds have awoken before their bodies and thus become suspended in a state between dreaming and reality. Legends are spawned from these nocturnal visitations and entities are forged.

"In Hmong culture, the Dab Tsog's visitations are not arbitrary; they are believed to be linked to spiritual or psychological disturbances within individuals. Those who have offended the spirits, neglected cultural rituals, or are weakened spiritually are more likely to encounter this malevolent being. These encounters, therefore, carry significant spiritual and psychological implications for the individuals involved.

"The Dab Tsog's appearance is elusive and variable, often reflecting the fears and cultural context of those it visits. While it may take on a more humanlike form to embody malice and decay, its animal forms could symbolize predatory instincts and stealth. These forms are not just physical manifestations but are imbued with symbolic meaning within Hmong culture.

"As a pressing spirit, the Dab Tsog's act of perching upon the chests of its victims symbolizes oppression and unseen burdens: unresolved guilt, stress, or ancestral debts. The sensation of being crushed or paralyzed during these encounters is not just physical. It can also be interpreted as an emotional or spiritual affliction, further emphasizing the symbolic nature of the Dab Tsog's actions.

"The Dab Tsog are believed to prefer males, which could be rooted in cultural beliefs about gender roles and spiritual responsibilities within the Hmong community. Males, often seen as the spiritual heads of households, could likewise

Similar Creatures in Folklore

Night Hag/Old Hag

GLOBAL

This entity is known in various cultures to cause sleep paralysis. It sits upon the chest of the sleeper, leading to nightmares. The feeling of being crushed or suffocated during sleep is often attributed to this malevolent presence.

Mora/Mara

THE BALKANS

A spirit from Balkan mythology, the mora is associated with nightmares and sleep paralysis. It is believed to visit sleepers at night, sitting on their chests and causing a feeling of breathlessness and terror.

Lilith

ANCIENT SUMER

Stemming from ancient Mesopotamian legends, Lilith is associated with the Lilītu, a class of female demons or wind spirits. She represents a dark force, often depicted as a seductive but dangerous entity that preys on men and children.

Kanashibari

JAPAN

In Japanese folklore, kanashibari refers to the phenomenon of sleep paralysis. It is described as an experience where an invisible force holds a person down in their sleep, often accompanied by a feeling of pressure on the chest and the presence of a dark figure.

Pesanta

CATALONIA, SPAIN

The pesanta is a feared creature in Catalan folklore, often appearing as a heavy black dog or cat that sits on the chests of sleepers to induce nightmares and an inability to move, characteristic of sleep paralysis.

Jinn

MIDDLE EAST

In Middle Eastern folklore, jinn are supernatural creatures that can cause sleep paralysis by sitting on the sleeper's chest. They are often described as shape-shifters that can appear in various forms.

be viewed as having a more significant spiritual burden that makes them more prone to such supernatural experiences.

"The Dab Tsog shares its lineage with the mare of Nordic myth or the cursed hag. She rides the chests of the sleeping and spins nightmares into their dreams. To be 'hag-ridden' is to experience the quintessence of fear. Vivid encounters like these, as haunting as they are intangible, may have given rise to the legend of the Dab Tsog.

"The Dab Tsog is among the most ancient fears that continue to haunt humanity's collective consciousness, an aide-mémoire to the mysteries of sleep. They are the guardians of the liminal threshold. They keep the key to the gate that separates waking life from the unfathomable depths of the dream world. And as long as sleep holds its secrets, the Dab Tsog will ride the night.

"Seek out the shamans, those versed in the old ways, for their wisdom forms a barrier against the predatory spirit. Secure your resting place and establish a good pattern of sleep, and these practices shall serve as your armor. Heed these words, wanderer, for they are not mere whispers on the wind but sacred rites from the ancients.

"In the lore passed down at Hmong firesides, the Dab Tsog preys not upon the feminine soul. If you dress as a woman, you may confound the phantom and it may overlook you, sparing you from its torment. Let this knowledge guide you. Let it be the cloak that shields you from the unseen and may your path be untouched by this entity's grasp.

"My dear companion, the Dab Tsog transcends the realm of folklore. It represents the threat of the unknown, a manifestation of fear, and the sudden grip of the night that transforms your fate. Beware the weight of worry and stress, for it weaves a thick web that ensnares the spirit, constricting all hope. It is the silent thief of joy, the shade that darkens the brightest of days."

They Spoke of Nightmares

1977 TO 1982, MINNESOTA, UNITED STATES

In 1977, a silhouette of dread fell over the Hmong community in the USA. Men, robust and in the prime of their lives, would succumb to an invisible predator. These men, whose average age was thirty-three, were the picture of health—yet they were dying unexpectedly in large numbers. In the year 1981 alone, twenty-six souls were lost to this nocturnal thief, most of them refugees seeking peace but instead finding a cruel fate.

In the stillness of a moonless evening, a strong, spirited young man retired to his bed, unaware that this night would be his last. As the community slept, a sinister silence crept through the air, a prelude to the horror that was about to spread. The man awoke to a suffocating darkness and a pressure on his chest so immense it was as if the very shadows sought to crush his soul. His breaths came in jagged gasps. The room spun, and the walls closed in; a figure loomed in the corner—an evil specter, the Dab Tsog, its eyes glinting bright with malice.

Paralyzed with fear, he could only watch as the creature drew closer, its form shifting and distorting in the dark. It advanced like a wraith woven from the dark contours of a nightmare. It was a silhouette against the lesser darkness. In a throaty, staccato croak, it spoke—a litany of despair, of lives unlived, and of the yawning abyss that awaited. Its voice was the death rattle of the world and the sound of old bones clacking together in a rhythm as ancient as time. The man's heart raced, a frantic drumbeat in his chest, heralding his end as the Dab Tsog's icy grip tightened, freezing the scream in his throat.

The room fell quiet as the Dab Tsog paused its invocation. It loomed over him, its breath a frigid whisper in the stillness, and hissed, "Mortal, behold your fears as they are fabricated by your own trembling hands. Gaze upon the void that gapes. It is ever hungry and looms at the edge of your feeble light. I am the silence that swallows your cries."

Its words slithered through the air, promising an eternity of darkness. The man, who was caught in the vicelike grip of terror, felt the essence of his nightmares given voice by this ancient specter. With a final, desperate plea, he sought the comfort of light and stretched frantically for the bedside lamp, but it was too late. The Dab Tsog caressed the man with a venomous embrace as his screams were devoured by the night. Come morning, his relatives found his lifeless form. His face and body lay twisted in terror.

This latest victim of the Dab Tsog was an ordinary soul caught in an ancient struggle between the forces of light and darkness.

What the medical community would eventually call Sudden Unexpected Nocturnal Death Syndrome (SUNDS) claimed the lives of many Hmong people. This mysterious condition, which often struck healthy young men during sleep, left families and communities grappling with grief and seeking answers. By the time the outbreak ended in the 1980s, over one hundred deaths were attributed to SUNDS.

Dream Demons:
The Haunting Origins of "Nightmare"

The etymology of the word "nightmare" traces back to the Old English term "mare," which referred to a mythological demon or goblin. This creature was believed to torment individuals with frightening dreams and often caused a feeling of suffocation. The word "mare" in this context is not related to the Modern English word for a female horse, but instead comes from the Proto-Germanic "Maron," which means "goblin" or "incubus."

The prefix "night" was later added to emphasize that these demonic visitations occurred at night. Over time, the term evolved from describing the supernatural being itself to the suffocating sensation it causes and, eventually, to any bad dream or distressing experience. This shift in meaning occurred around the mid-sixteenth century. The term "nightmare" is related to the Dutch "nachtmerrie" and the German "Nachtmahr," which also have their roots in folklore and describe similar nocturnal spirits associated with bad dreams.

The word "nightmare" now refers to any frightening dream. Still, its origins remind us of a time when the human mind explained unfathomable things through the lens of malevolent entities.

The Cry of La Llorona

EL ÁRBOL DEL TULE

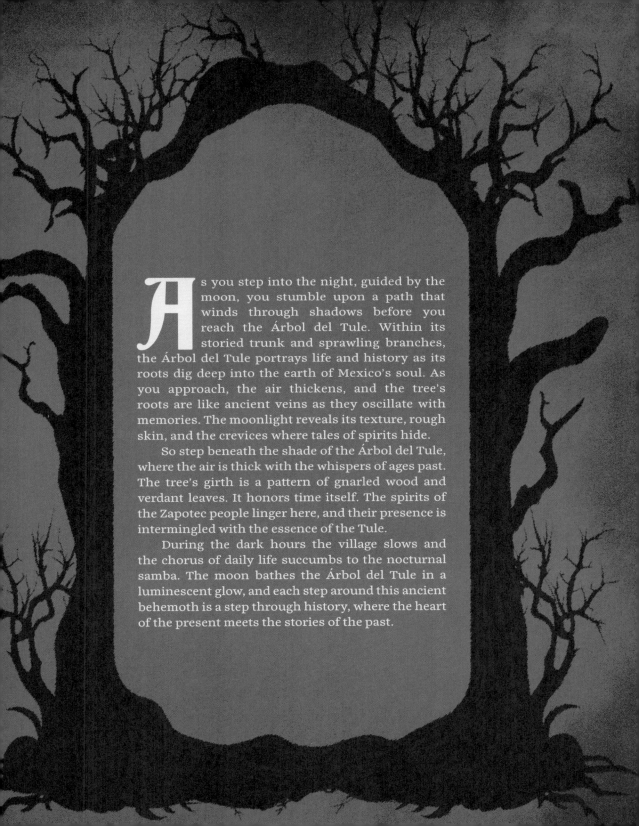

As you step into the night, guided by the moon, you stumble upon a path that winds through shadows before you reach the Árbol del Tule. Within its storied trunk and sprawling branches, the Árbol del Tule portrays life and history as its roots dig deep into the earth of Mexico's soul. As you approach, the air thickens, and the tree's roots are like ancient veins as they oscillate with memories. The moonlight reveals its texture, rough skin, and the crevices where tales of spirits hide.

So step beneath the shade of the Árbol del Tule, where the air is thick with the whispers of ages past. The tree's girth is a pattern of gnarled wood and verdant leaves. It honors time itself. The spirits of the Zapotec people linger here, and their presence is intermingled with the essence of the Tule.

During the dark hours the village slows and the chorus of daily life succumbs to the nocturnal samba. The moon bathes the Árbol del Tule in a luminescent glow, and each step around this ancient behemoth is a step through history, where the heart of the present meets the stories of the past.

Y ou lean gently against the colossal trunk of the Árbol del Tule, its ancient grooves and knots forming a natural seat around you. The tree, known for its remarkable girth and longevity, embraces you with its history. "La Llorona," it calls, "is the quintessence of a mother's grief. She is a cry in the night full of misery and suffering.

"Ushered in with the twilight silhouettes, the tale of La Llorona emerges from the collective soul of the Mexican people. It is a legend marinated in an ancient culture's heartache. It has crossed borders and generations and found a home in the hearts of the Chicano and Latin American communities, where it is passed down like a precious heirloom darkened with the patina of time.

"La Llorona is a terrifying phantom born from the depths of despair. She is the Weeping Woman, a ghostly figure robed in a tattered gown that clings to her emaciated frame and is stained by the murky waters she haunts. Her long and unkempt hair writhes like serpents; her once warm and loving eyes are now hollow, blackened sockets. She cries eternally, her tears carving rivulets of decay down her pallid cheeks.

"Her arms are elongated and skeletal. They stretch forth with sinewy veins pulsating beneath translucent skin. Her hands, gnarled talons with nails darkened and jagged, bear the stains of her heinous act. Once tender with maternal love, these hands are now clenched into fists of rage, reaching out to tear at your soul.

"Long ago, she was a woman of flesh and blood. Her heart had brimmed with the purest kind of love that blossomed in the warmth of her children's laughter and the tender embrace of her partner. Her life was full of joyous moments, but fate shredded her happiness with its cruel and fickle ways and the painful grip of betrayal struck deep.

"Her partner, who was once her confidante and companion, succumbed to the seductress's call of temptation. He left La Llorona and their children for another woman. This betrayal became a poison seeping into her veins, clouding her mind with a darkness corrupted by lies and deceit.

"In a tragic twist, wrought from the depths of her madness, she led her children to the water's edge. There, where the river kissed the shore, she surrendered to the malevolent chorus in her mind. With trembling hands and a heart shattered into a thousand pieces, she held her children under the water and watched impassively as their innocent eyes grew wide with confusion and fear.

"As the waters stilled and the night reclaimed its silence, the gravity of her grievous deed crashed upon her like the waves upon the rocks. Consumed by

Similar Creatures in Folklore

Banshee
IRELAND

A female spirit whose wail is said to forewarn the death of a family member. She is often envisioned as an old woman in rags with long, flowing hair and eyes red from crying.

Pontianak
MALAYSIA/INDONESIA

The ghost of a woman who died while giving birth and now seeks retribution. Her presence is often announced by baby cries or feminine wails.

Churel (page 117)
SOUTH ASIA

The churel is the ghost of a woman who died while giving birth or in some unjust manner. She is known to wail and is associated with bad omens.

Cihuateteo
MEXICO

The cihuateteos are ghosts of women who died while giving birth. They return to the earth as malevolent spirits, often accompanied by sounds of wailing, to steal children.

Bean Nighe
SCOTLAND

A woman observed cleaning the bloodstained clothing of people about to perish. Her wails are considered an omen of death.

Rusalka
SLAVIC FOLKLORE

Water nymphs or ghosts of young women who died from brutal or premature deaths. They shriek or sing in an effort to entice men to their deaths.

Acheri
OJIBWE

The ghost of a young girl who brings illness to children with her mournful cries from mountaintops.

Aswang
THE PHILIPPINES

A shape-shifting monster that wails to signal its presence. It preys on pregnant women and can take on various forms.

La Sayona
VENEZUELA

A vengeful spirit of a woman who was deceived by her husband. She is known to wail and seeks to punish unfaithful men.

the weight of her actions, her spirit fractured and left behind a shell haunted by dreams of her children's cries.

"Her spirit lingers, a ghostly form bound to the water's edge. She roams eternally and the mournful dirge of her wails chills the bones of those who hear it. She traverses the banks, searching for her children, reaching out to the void, hoping to clasp the warmth of the lives she extinguished.

"Her mourning is perpetual, a cycle with no end. For her, there is no solace, no redemption—only the eternal torment of a mother who became the architect of her own sorrow. And so, she wanders as a specter of loss and pain, a reminder of the fragility of joy and the depths to which the human soul can fall.

"She is known for her mournful wailing: '¡Ay, mis hijos!' ('Oh, my children!'), which she cries as she wanders near bodies of water. Her presence is said to bring misfortune and she is feared by children in particular, whom she is believed to be drawn to, mistaking them for her own.

"The folklore of La Llorona draws in part from the Aztec peoples' beliefs in spirits and the supernatural as a way to understand and explain the world around them. Her story may be linked to Indigenous tales of water spirits or goddesses, such as the Aztec goddess Chalchiuhtlicue, who was associated with water and was believed to drown people. This connection to water and nature reflects a reverence for the land and its elements, which was central to Aztec spirituality and worldview.

"Wanderer, venture lightly by the water's edge, for it is there that La Llorona lingers. Though she is often seen as a vengeful wraith, her tale is one of complexity. In the whispers of folk magic, she is sometimes felicitated as a protector, her image a bulwark against wickedness and a fire of fortune for women and the young.

"Invoking her grace and protection may be wise in the rites of old. Yet she is a dreaded phantom in modern lore, eternally seeking children to call her own. Beware her sorrowful call and let not curiosity draw you near, for her cry leads the less diligent into the depths of her mournful embrace.

"Listen closely, my newfound companion. To ignore this counsel is to court peril. La Llorona is far beyond a legend. She also personifies the weight of women's societal shackles—the silent sadness borne through generations."

And Then She Floated

SEPTEMBER 2016, MEXICO CITY, MEXICO

In the muted light of Mexico City, where the clamor of the day relented to the caress of night, Juan brushed against the eternal grief that had seeped into the soil of this land. The moon was a quiet observer as it hung low in the sky. Its luminescent aura cast everything in a silvery hue, a sight that filled the young man with wonder and awe.

Juan was at a crossroads when his gaze was drawn to a figure standing in the road. Her form blurred at the edges, and her hair, as dark as a raven's wing, cascaded over her shoulders. She stood unmoving on the crosswalk with a freakish stillness that belied the chaos of life around her.

A chill that was not of the night air crept up Juan's spine, a primal warning that the vision before him was not of this world. Cars passed, their headlights slicing through the darkness and cutting right through her, leaving her form untouched. Juan struggled to reconcile the figure with the world he knew—a world of certainty and order.

The air grew colder still. It was a frost born not of temperature but of terror. As Juan stood transfixed, the apparition before him began to transform. Her arms now reached out toward him with a slow, deliberate movement that seemed to contradict the flow of time. The sleeves of her white garment fell back to reveal limbs that were a scene of terror: skin pale as moonlight, marred by the crimson stain of wounds long past, and veins like dark rivers mapped across her flesh.

Her hands trembled, and she reached for Juan in a desperation that spoke of centuries of heartbreak. Her fingers, marred with the evidence of her tragic tale, seemed to claw at an invisible barrier that separated her world from his. Her neck cricked to the side, and then she wailed with a sound that tore through the silence like a rending of the heavens.

With her form now elongated, the ghostly figure stood poised on tiptoes. The cracked asphalt beneath her feet seemed to writhe as if recoiling in disgust from her touch.

And then she floated.

It was not a gentle ascent but a sinister glide. The figure's feet barely grazed the ground as if she were suspended by invisible strings. The wraith's eyes were hollow, unblinking, and bore into Juan's soul.

Closer still.

Juan's heart raced. He tried to run, but his limbs betrayed him. The ghostly image drew closer, and her skeletal fingers were rimmed with frost as they brushed against his cheek. Her lips moved in a jittery, soundless whisper that clawed at his sanity.

And then, with a final, agonizing flow, she was upon him. Her face twisted in anguish.

Her mouth was a chasm of darkness that opened impossibly wide from which her lamentation poured forth. It was as though the night had been drawn into her being, a vortex that threatened to consume all light, all hope.

Then her wails diminished into whispers, and her form became even less defined. Finally, her presence dissipated. La Llorona was extinguished, leaving behind a silence that pressed against Juan's ears. He stood alone at the crosswalk. Once again, the night was just a night, and the streetlights were just illuminations in the dark.

Lullaby of Doom:
The Crying Call of La Lechuza

La Lechuza is another figure from Mexican folklore, often described as a large owl with the face of an old woman. According to the legend, La Lechuza is a witch who transforms into an owl and preys on those who wander at night. Some stories hint that she was once a human who became a vengeful entity after some kind of tragedy or injustice.

But what is truly chilling in many tales is that La Lechuza emits the sound of a crying baby to lure victims outside, only to snatch them away to her lair. But beware, for it is said that merely seeing La Lechuza is an omen of bad luck or death. The lore varies by region, with some believing that harming La Lechuza could also harm the human linked to it. Special prayers might reveal La Lechuza's true identity.

The Ijiraq Among Us

THE BALSAM POPLAR TREE

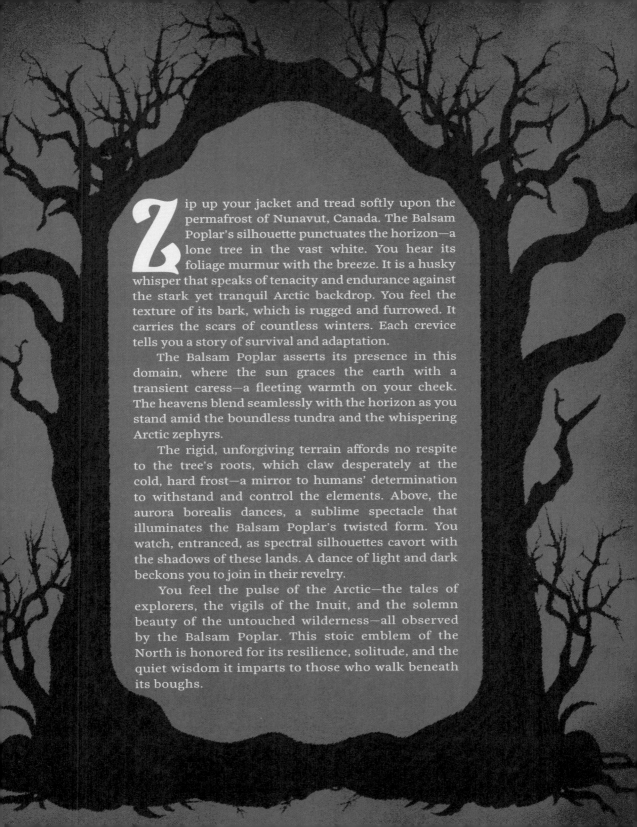

Zip up your jacket and tread softly upon the permafrost of Nunavut, Canada. The Balsam Poplar's silhouette punctuates the horizon—a lone tree in the vast white. You hear its foliage murmur with the breeze. It is a husky whisper that speaks of tenacity and endurance against the stark yet tranquil Arctic backdrop. You feel the texture of its bark, which is rugged and furrowed. It carries the scars of countless winters. Each crevice tells you a story of survival and adaptation.

The Balsam Poplar asserts its presence in this domain, where the sun graces the earth with a transient caress—a fleeting warmth on your cheek. The heavens blend seamlessly with the horizon as you stand amid the boundless tundra and the whispering Arctic zephyrs.

The rigid, unforgiving terrain affords no respite to the tree's roots, which claw desperately at the cold, hard frost—a mirror to humans' determination to withstand and control the elements. Above, the aurora borealis dances, a sublime spectacle that illuminates the Balsam Poplar's twisted form. You watch, entranced, as spectral silhouettes cavort with the shadows of these lands. A dance of light and dark beckons you to join in their revelry.

You feel the pulse of the Arctic—the tales of explorers, the vigils of the Inuit, and the solemn beauty of the untouched wilderness—all observed by the Balsam Poplar. This stoic emblem of the North is honored for its resilience, solitude, and the quiet wisdom it imparts to those who walk beneath its boughs.

Y ou edge closer, the crunch of snow beneath your boots breaking the silence of the Arctic expanse, and press your ear against the Balsam Poplar. It stands proud and pertinacious in this frozen place. The chill of the bark seeps into your skin as it begins to speak. Its gravelly voice resonates deeply, a soft yet clear articulation.

"The Ijiraq," it begins, "embodies the Arctic's deepest fears. Born from the land's whiteness, it teaches lessons of respect and caution. In the twilight's chill where the aurora whispers, the Ijiraq's (or Ijiraat) ruby eyes release a fiery flicker. It is the conjuror of the Arctic's hidden tales, its essence a shroud that beckons forth the soul and mind. Its legend is spun from Inuit qiviut yarns—the velvety undercoat of the muskox. It is a story of deception and spectral allure.

"The word 'Ijiraq'—plural form Ijirait—is from the North Baffin dialect and means 'shape-shifter.' These beings are woven intricately into Inuit culture, embodying the perils and trepidations of the Arctic wilds. They are the tales told to caution the careless, the narratives that bind the community with shared fears and warnings. Approach their lore with respect and caution, for they are not to be trifled with.

"With forms as fluid as the northern lights, the Ijiraq's presence is elusive, a fleeting glimpse just out of sight: a strange caribou, or a silhouetted figure with eyes and mouth askew and red eyes that pierce the pristine white terrain. Amid the ice and the endless night, its form shifts, a menagerie of the Arctic's children, yet is marked always by the crimson stare that betrays its true nature.

"Ijirait are the silhouettes that haunt the fringes of the mind and hunt the lost and the young. They often disguise themselves as part of the Arctic environment, masquerading as innocuous elements of their frigid domain—formations such as rocks or icebergs, only revealing their real form to those they deem worthy.

"Their true terror lies not in physical predation but in the theft of memories, a chilling act that they perform by plucking them from your mind and devouring them much as snowflakes melt on your tongue. To the solitary wanderer, they bring a fracture in time, a blurring of faces, a dissolving of names, and in their wake they leave a husk haunted by the traces of what once was. The Ijirait define solitude. Their hunt is a game of shadows and mimicry. Their maleficence is a subtle curse, a theft of the past's warmth, leaving their prey adrift in a sea of fragmented recollections and ghostly whispers.

"The Ijirait glide. Their touch is a brush with the void and a bargain struck in the cold—a choice between oblivion and the haunting of half-remembered dreams. The inukshuk that dot the landscape usher lost souls, urging them to reclaim what was stolen. But the Ijirait are cunning. They resist, clinging to their cache of memories. Only the bravest—those who dare to confront their forgotten past—can

Similar Creatures in Folklore

Nagual

MESOAMERICAN FOLKLORE

Throughout Mesoamerican folklore, the nagual is seen as a bulwark against evil spirits. Individuals are believed to have an animal spirit counterpart—a nagual can transform into this animal form. This transformation is often associated with powerful spiritual insight and is linked to the Mesoamerican calendrical system used for divination.

Púca / Pooka (page 141)

IRELAND

The púca, from Celtic folklore, is a shape-shifter that can bring fortune or misfortune. It can transform into various animals and is often associated with agriculture, as it can either help or hinder rural communities. The Púca is also known to possess humanlike intelligence and may offer cryptic advice.

Selkie (page 133)

SCOTLAND AND IRELAND

In Scottish and Irish mythology, selkies are sea creatures that can slip out of their skin and walk on land as humans. These beings are often depicted in tales involving romantic relationships with humans and possess the tragic ability to be coerced into human marriages by someone who steals their seal skin.

Kitsune

JAPAN

In Japanese folklore, the kitsune is a revered fox spirit. It is considered highly intelligent and capable of magic, including shape-shifting abilities. The kitsune are associated with the deity Inari, the protector god of rice cultivation, and are seen as messengers between the earthly and celestial empires.

Berserker

NORSE MYTHOLOGY

Many Old Norse sources mention berserkers, who were renowned for their skill in battle and fought with a trancelike fury, often without armor. Some legends claim that berserkers derived their battle strength through a spiritual connection to bears, wolves, and wild boars.

Yee Naaldlooshii (Skinwalker) (pages 125 and 141)

NAVAJO

A skinwalker is an evil witch who can change into, take on the form of, or pass for an animal in Navajo culture. They are the antithesis of Navajo cultural values and are feared for their malevolent magic and manipulative abilities.

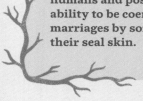

pry open the Ijiraq's frostbitten fingers. In their role as guideposts for the Inuit, the inukshuk can lead these brave souls home, but they can only do so much. The rest is up to the individual's courage and determination.

"Some elders contend that the Ijirait are not inherently malevolent but simply misunderstood. Some caution that these beings are mirages, suggesting that when distant mountains or islands appear unnaturally large or close, the Ijirait may be near. Still others believe the Ijirait may manifest to deliver messages to wayfarers.

"The lore of the Ijiraq is intertwined deeply with the Inuit respect for and understanding of their homeland. It reflects a world where nothing is static and everything is interconnected—the land, the weather, the animals, and the people. The Ijirait are thought to possess an intimate knowledge of this land, moving through it with a grace that belies their size and strength.

"These beings are not just fabrications of imagination but serve as a metaphor for the ever-changing conditions of the Arctic. They represent the idea that what one sees may not always be what it seems. The shifting ice can reveal treacherous waters beneath; a seemingly solid surface may give way without warning. The Ijiraq reminds the Inuit of the need for precaution and regard for nature's strength.

"Inhabiting the threshold between our world and the spirit realm, the Ijirait hold a significant role as protectors of ancient wisdom. They carry within them stories of generations past, serving as a vital link to ancestral knowledge. Their presence in folklore is a constant reminder to honor traditions and foster a deep connection with one's heritage. In many cultures, memories are considered integral to a person's identity and a connection to community and environment. The act of stealing memories by a creature like the Ijiraq could symbolize losing one's identity or disconnecting from one's cultural heritage and the territory one inhabits.

"In a land where daylight and darkness reign in extremes, where the aurora borealis paints the sky in a vibrant array of color, the Ijirait are symbols of adaptability and survival. They are revered not only out of fear but also out of admiration for their mastery over an environment that demands respect and resilience.

"Thus, in the heart of the Arctic, among the whispering winds and beneath the watchful gaze of the northern lights, the Ijirait continue their vigil—ever present and ever elusive.

"Traveler of the tundra, let wisdom be your compass and prudence your guide. To shield yourself from the Ijirait, it is wise to heed the land and maintain a respectful berth from the areas they roam. Their artifice is as deep as the snow and their guile shifts continually like the aurora borealis. They are not just shape-shifters, but masters of illusion and can blend seamlessly into their surroundings and deceive even the most vigilant of observers. In this ever-changing landscape, engage with the locals, share stories, and listen intently. This communion of experiences will anchor your memories and ensure they remain with you as steadfastly as the northern stars.

"If needed, seek the counsel of shamans, those keepers of ancient rites, for they hold the keys to unraveling the Ijiraq's deceptions. Let this lore be your lantern in the twilight, traveler, and may your journey be free from the Ijiraq's spectral snares.

"And so, my friend, when the Arctic whispers its warnings: Beware the Ijirait, for they steal more than flesh and bone. They pilfer the very essence of who you are— the memories that shape you, the stories that bind you. To encounter them is to risk losing yourself forever."

What Devilry Is This?

MAY 1845 TO 1846,
KING WILLIAM ISLAND, NUNAVUT, CANADA

The HMS *Terror* and HMS *Erebus* embarked on the Franklin Expedition in 1845 to chart the elusive Northwest Passage. Under the command of Sir John Franklin, the ships were the pinnacle of naval engineering, fortified against the ice and equipped with provisions for three years.

As they sailed from London down the River Thames, optimism was high among the 128 officers and men. The ships were last seen by Europeans in Baffin Bay off the coast of Greenland before they vanished into the icy unknown.

The expedition was anchored at Beechey Island during the winter of 1845 to 1846, and three members perished. The explorers traveled down Peel Sound the following summer, but in September 1846 got stuck in ice off King William Island. The crew endured the Arctic's merciless conditions, with dwindling supplies and encroaching ice. The ships were designed to withstand such pressures, but they were locked fast.

In the relentless cold of the Arctic, the crew of HMS *Terror* found themselves prisoners of the ice, and the ships had become their jails.

"Keep your eyes sharp, lads," Crozier commanded as his breath froze, leaving a frigid ghost in the air. "The land can play tricks on the mind."

"Aye, Captain," replied Lieutenant Little, his gaze piercing the white expanse. "But it's not the ice alone that troubles the men. It's the tales of the Ijirait. The locals say they wear the faces of men."

As the Arctic day waned, a figure appeared on the horizon, moving with an eerie grace.

"There! What devilry is this?" cried a young midshipman, his finger trembling as he pointed.

Crozier squinted, discerning the outline of the figure. "Steady, boy. It's the hunger and the cold. They conjure phantoms."

But the figure drew nearer. The crew watched in mute horror as it took the shape of a man they knew, a man who had perished months before.

"James?" whispered a sailor, his voice barely carrying over the howling wind as the ship creaked ominously beneath him.

The apparition spoke, its voice devoid of warmth. "You cannot escape the hunger nor my cold embrace."

Crozier stepped forward, his resolve steeling him against the fear that clawed at his heart. "You are not James. Reveal yourself, spirit!"

The figure chuckled, a sound that seemed to come from the ice itself, a sinister calling of cracks and groans. "I am what you fear and what you will never fully comprehend."

Suddenly, the figure began to scuttle—its movements came erratic and swift, like a spider skittering across the ice. Its form blurred and shifted between man and shade as if honed from the darkness of a storm.

Crozier's breath caught in his throat as the figure loomed closer, its eyes glinting with a malevolent red light. "I am the ravenous void, the abyss that stares back at you. I am the deathly silence that will consume you."

The sailor's heart pounded with horror as the figure reached out with hands that were not hands, but tendrils of mist and frost. "And you," it hissed, "are mine."

The crew stood transfixed as the narrow wall between reality and lore tumbled down around them. In the end, both *Terror* and *Erebus* were abandoned, and the surviving crew members vanished into the frozen wilderness.

Beneath the Ice: The Qalupalik, an Arctic Cautionary Tale

In Inuit folklore, the Qalupalik are formidable creatures that reside beneath the icy surface of the sea. These beings may seem strangely familiar, with their humanlike appearance, long hair, green skin, and elongated nails. Their presence in folklore is a cautionary tale, warning children to steer clear of the water's edge or thin ice.

The Howl of Werewolves

YGGDRASIL

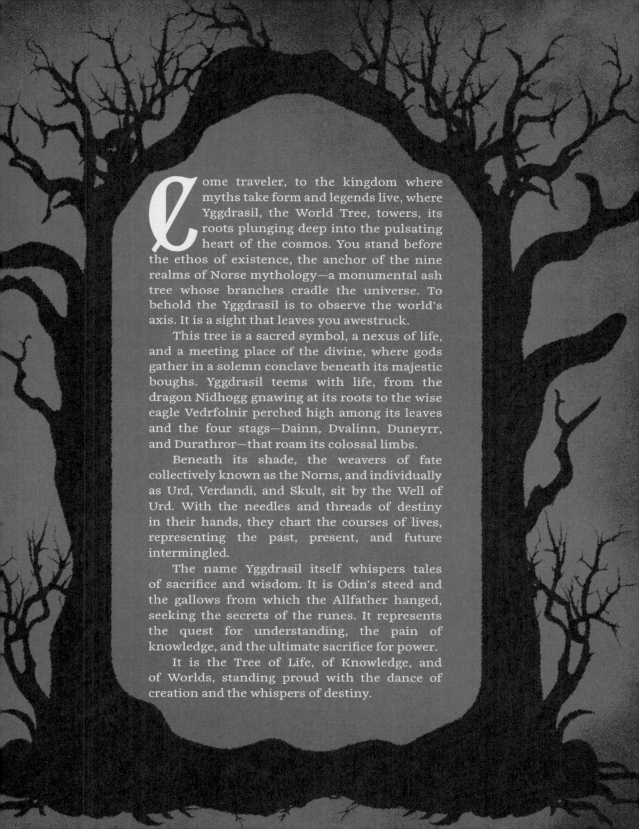

Come traveler, to the kingdom where myths take form and legends live, where Yggdrasil, the World Tree, towers, its roots plunging deep into the pulsating heart of the cosmos. You stand before the ethos of existence, the anchor of the nine realms of Norse mythology—a monumental ash tree whose branches cradle the universe. To behold the Yggdrasil is to observe the world's axis. It is a sight that leaves you awestruck.

This tree is a sacred symbol, a nexus of life, and a meeting place of the divine, where gods gather in a solemn conclave beneath its majestic boughs. Yggdrasil teems with life, from the dragon Nidhogg gnawing at its roots to the wise eagle Vedrfolnir perched high among its leaves and the four stags—Dainn, Dvalinn, Duneyrr, and Durathror—that roam its colossal limbs.

Beneath its shade, the weavers of fate collectively known as the Norns, and individually as Urd, Verdandi, and Skult, sit by the Well of Urd. With the needles and threads of destiny in their hands, they chart the courses of lives, representing the past, present, and future intermingled.

The name Yggdrasil itself whispers tales of sacrifice and wisdom. It is Odin's steed and the gallows from which the Allfather hanged, seeking the secrets of the runes. It represents the quest for understanding, the pain of knowledge, and the ultimate sacrifice for power.

It is the Tree of Life, of Knowledge, and of Worlds, standing proud with the dance of creation and the whispers of destiny.

Y ou step into the dusky hollows of this gargantuan tree where legend and truth tangle. Above, Yggdrasil's branches cradle the cosmos, while the Norns weave your fate below. The tree hums with an ancient power, a call of life and destiny. It speaks with a voice like tumbling leaves in a timeless dance. "Within me dwells the distillate of worlds, the breath of the universe," Yggdrasil murmurs. "And before you, the Werewolf—my child of the night, a spirit of both shadow and light.

"In the depths of the dark forest, the Werewolf surreptitiously stalks, a creature born from the melding of man and beast. Its beginnings are shrouded in the ancient myths of Europe, where it first emerged in Greek and Roman lore. The Werewolf, or lycanthrope, has since plagued the collective nightmares of civilizations, an oblique allegory of untamed nature let loose.

"The word 'Werewolf,' derived from the Old English *werwulf*, means 'man-wolf.' These beings run deep in the veins of folklore of many cultures, embodying the primal fears of the wilds. In Norse mythology, the Fenrir wolf is a prominent figure, while Greek mythology is famous for the tale of Lycaon, who saw Zeus change him into a wolf. They are the tales whispered to warn and the narratives that bond communities with shared fear and caution.

"The transformation of the Werewolf from man to monster is an oozing spectacle of horror. Flesh warps and bones crack in a cacophony of pain. Once turned, the Werewolf becomes a maelstrom of violence, a whirlwind of claws and teeth that knows neither friend, family, nor foe, only the voracious lust for destruction. Its muscles bulge with unnatural strength and its matted fur emits a putrid stench that chokes you. Its eyes are ablaze with a feral glow, revealing a terrifying, cunning intelligence with jaws that could snap steel and claws that have mercilessly torn apart countless victims.

"The lore of the Werewolf is more nuanced, and it is a complex creature of folklore and myth. Not all are deemed malevolent, as some tales speak of benevolent lycanthropes. These beasts represent the cursed or damned man archetype, who guard the innocent and seek redemption. Their affliction is a cruel twist of fate rather than a mark of evil.

"The Werewolves' howls cut through the silence in the forest's gloom, where even the glowing moon dares not tread. The moon plays a significant role in Werewolf folklore, believed to be the source of their power and the trigger for their transformation. They are the night's dark lunatics! Now come yowl at the moon, traveler. It really is quite liberating!

"Legends whisper that the Werewolf's curse was born from forbidden pacts and heinous crimes against nature. Perhaps it was a divine retribution, a reflection of

Similar Creatures in Folklore

Weretiger
CHINA

In Chinese mythology, weretigers are believed to be humans who can transform into tigers, a process sometimes attributed to the magical power of the tiger or divine intervention. They symbolize willpower, courage, and personal strength and are seen as spiritual beings embodying the drive to achieve and progress in the material world.

Werehyena
HORN OF AFRICA REGION

The myth of the werehyena is prevalent in the folklore of the Horn of Africa, including Ethiopia, Somalia, and Sudan. It is reported that these animals may change shape at whim with the use of a magic stick or ash sprinkler. Sometimes their metamorphosis is triggered simply by the smell of human flesh. They are often associated with grave robbing and are viewed with suspicion and dread.

Varcolac
ROMANIA

In Romanian legend, the varcolac is sometimes depicted as a creature that can consume the sun and moon, causing eclipses. It is also believed to be a wizard who can take a wolf's form and roam the night during lunar phases.

Loup-Garou
FRANCE

A well-known creature in French folklore, the loup-garou is akin to the Werewolf. It is said that if a person does not confess to a priest at least once a year, they become vulnerable to becoming a loup-garou.

Lupo Mannaro
ITALY

Like the loup-garou, the lupo mannaro is an Italian variant of the Werewolf, a person who transforms into a wolf due to a curse or affliction.

the savagery lurking within all men, or an affliction transmitted through bite and blood. This contagious malignance preys on the weak-willed—a curse that, once suffered, can never be undone.

"Medical conditions that cause physical or mental abnormalities, excessive hair growth, porphyria (sensitivity to sunlight and skin lesions), or rabies (aggression and animallike behavior) may have a role in this lore. Moreover, serial killers or cannibals who committed horrific crimes and were accused of being in league with the devil or practicing witchcraft were seen as Werewolves in the trials of the Middle Ages. The motivations behind these trials—which occurred in many parts of Europe in the fifteenth, sixteenth, and seventeenth centuries—included superstition, conflicts between religion and politics, and the need to assign blame for difficult circumstances such as moral panics, unexplained illnesses, and natural disasters.

"The full moon's luminous presence in the tales of the Werewolf is connected deeply to its association with hunting. In times past, the full moon was a guide for venators navigating the dark wilderness, a time when prey was plentiful and the hunt was rich and red. Thus, the Werewolf's transformation under the full moon may symbolize the primal hunt, the awakening of an ancient predator driven by the same lunar force that once guided human hunters.

"The Werewolf is the embodiment of sheer terror. Its howl is a mournful requiem that pierces the silence of the dark woods, a chilling proem to impending carnage. To the lone traveler, it is a blurring of humanity and a revelation of the beast within. Werewolves epitomize the wild. Their hunt is a ritual of savagery and instinct and their fury is a raw force that manifests nature's unchecked ferocity.

"Werewolves' transformative curse speaks to humanity's deep-seated fear of the unknown—a reflection of an environment where one's form can betray you, where the beast is wrapped in sheep's clothing, and where the lunar cycle breaks the nuanced link between man and monster. It is not just a physical change but a symbolic one, representing the loss of control and the unleashing of primal instincts. Werewolves characterize humanity's unpredictable spirit—where a man's silhouette may contort with the moon's rise and the ground beneath one's feet may become a hunting ground. They are the children of the night, marked by the luminous stare that reveals their wild nature, and they are as much a part of the forest as the trees and the darkness.

"Seeker of the moonlit path, let these venerable verses illuminate your way. To shield yourself from the Werewolf's fury, one must embrace the sage knowledge shared through stories told by the candle's glow. Silver is the bane of the beast, a purifying element that can stop its rampage. A bullet or blade forged from this metal can pierce the Werewolf's cursed hide and end its reign of terror. Silver as a protective measure is a common theme in Werewolf folklore, believed to be effective due to its purity and association with the moon. Wolfsbane, too, is said to repel the creature. Its toxic blooms are a natural ward against this evil.

"So, dear sojourner, arm yourself with knowledge and silver, for the Werewolf is a manifestation of the beast within—a memento of the thin veneer that divides man from monster. In the dead of night, when the moon is full and bright, remember these words and pray that you do not hear the distant howl of the Werewolf, for it may be the last sound you ever hear. To walk the woods when the Werewolf roams is to dance with the Devil."

Maybe We Should Go Inside

MAY 2005, MAINE, UNITED STATES

One evening, Roger and Becky Heybyrne were sitting comfortably together on their porch when they noticed something amiss: pulsing lights reflecting off the forest's contorted tree trunks and foliage. Roger exchanged a glance with Becky, their unspoken words hanging heavy in the evening air.

Days later, the couple's daughter, Beth, and her boyfriend, Tyler, ventured into the ancient woodland. The dogs—loyal hounds of the Heybyrne family—caught a scent and raised their hackles. Their snouts led them unerringly toward an unnatural hole in the ground.

Beth peered into the abyss. The hollow's edges were scraggy as if gouged out by some large, hungry predator. Dread clawed at Beth's stomach as Tyler peered into the hole. He hesitated.

"Tyler," Beth murmured, "We should go back. I'm scared."

Together, they hurried back to the farmhouse. The dogs, too, retreated, their tails tucked between their legs.

Memorial Day weekend descended upon the Heybyrnes, and as Becky and Roger sat out on the porch, they felt the shift in the air.

Something was off, a dissonance that vibrated through the very timbers of their farmhouse. Roger glanced at Becky. "Maybe we should go inside?" He suggested, his voice low.

Becky, ever practical, hesitated. "What is it, Roger?"

"I don't know," he admitted. "Just a feeling."

A strange noise echoed from the woodland. It wasn't the typical rustle of foliage or the distant call of the night's denizens. It was primal, guttural—a sound that ripped at the edges of reality. Roger stepped to the porch's edge and peered out into the murky night.

And there they were: three sets of eyes, luminous and intense, piercing with an otherworldly glow. Giant, wolflike creatures stalked the garden with a predatory grace. Their silhouettes blurred, and they shifted between two legs and four. As the night deepened, the three pairs of eyes became five.

Becky gasped. "What are they?"

"I don't know," he whispered. "Get inside, now."

From inside the home, the couple watched the creatures move with dreadful fluidity. Roger tried to pull Becky away from the window, but her gaze remained glued on the unnatural visitors. "Roger," she said, trembling, "what do they want?"

Becky woke Beth from a deep sleep, and they peered through the window. One of the creatures, sensing their stare, rose on two legs. The behemoth's eyes locked with Becky's in challenge.

Together, the family fortified their home against the unknown. The creatures, however, were relentless. Their menacing and hungry growls penetrated the night. They were only kept at bay by the impenetrable energy of the porch light.

And so, the Heybyrnes waited as the monsters lingered. Morning brought relief, though their sanctuary was now marred by the memory of the previous night.

The creatures vanished. Their footprints, however, remained—proof of their passage.

Moonlit Terror: The Werewolf Trials of Sixteenth-Century France

Pierre Burgot and Michel Verdun were shepherds in France who were executed in 1521 for their supposed transformation into wolves. According to historical accounts, during a thunderstorm Burgot was approached by three black-clad horsemen who offered protection for his sheep and wealth in exchange for renouncing his faith and serving them. Both Burgot and Verdun later confessed to attending a witches' sabbath, where they were anointed with a substance that allowed them to assume wolflife forms and commit acts of violence.

Gilles Garnier, also known as the Hermit of St. Bonnot, was another Frenchman accused of lycanthropy. It was said that when children strayed too far from their homes, he would attack and devour them. His case contributed to the werewolf hysteria in France during the sixteenth century.

The Black Bird of Chernobyl

THE BLACKTHORN TREE

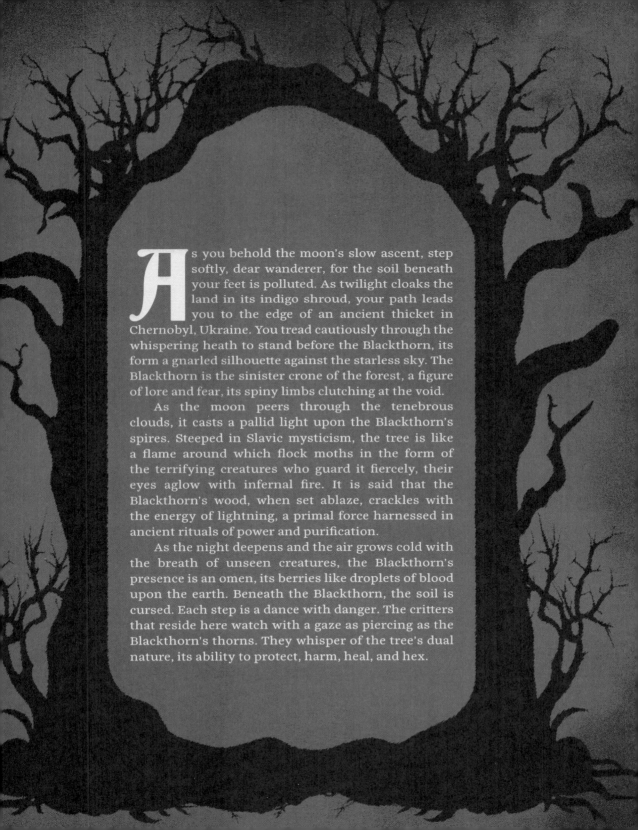

As you behold the moon's slow ascent, step softly, dear wanderer, for the soil beneath your feet is polluted. As twilight cloaks the land in its indigo shroud, your path leads you to the edge of an ancient thicket in Chernobyl, Ukraine. You tread cautiously through the whispering heath to stand before the Blackthorn, its form a gnarled silhouette against the starless sky. The Blackthorn is the sinister crone of the forest, a figure of lore and fear, its spiny limbs clutching at the void.

As the moon peers through the tenebrous clouds, it casts a pallid light upon the Blackthorn's spires. Steeped in Slavic mysticism, the tree is like a flame around which flock moths in the form of the terrifying creatures who guard it fiercely, their eyes aglow with infernal fire. It is said that the Blackthorn's wood, when set ablaze, crackles with the energy of lightning, a primal force harnessed in ancient rituals of power and purification.

As the night deepens and the air grows cold with the breath of unseen creatures, the Blackthorn's presence is an omen, its berries like droplets of blood upon the earth. Beneath the Blackthorn, the soil is cursed. Each step is a dance with danger. The critters that reside here watch with a gaze as piercing as the Blackthorn's thorns. They whisper of the tree's dual nature, its ability to protect, harm, heal, and hex.

Y ou trace the deep gouges on the Blackthorn. Each line is a tale scorched into the wood. Suddenly, a sound pierces the stillness—a cackle, dry and crackling like the branches themselves. "The curses, oh the curses!" the Blackthorn tree exclaims with glee. "Each mark upon my bark, a spell of old, a hex bound tight with a witch's hold."

The Blackthorn's leaves shiver with mirth. "Beware, dear traveler, for my thorns are sharp and my curses are many. A prick of blood, a whispered chant, and your fate is sealed under the moon's slant."

You retract your hand sharply. The Blackthorn, the spiteful keeper of lore, imparts its story with a resonance that frightens you deeply.

"The Black Bird of Chernobyl," it chuckles, "is an incarnation of the land's deepest fears and darkest moments. These are complicated creatures born from the shades of forewarning, teaching a lesson against ignorance and neglect.

"In the days leading up to the catastrophic nuclear accident, workers at the Chernobyl plant whispered of a horrifying creature. Described as a large, black bird devoid of a head, with gigantic wings and fiery red eyes, it was a sight that burrowed its way into the sleep of many. This cryptid is the Black Bird of Chernobyl, also called the Chernobyl Mothman.

"Born from the depths of the unknown, this beast emerges as a symbol of Chernobyl's haunting legacy. It is a creature of myth and a manifestation of dread—a watcher of the forsaken, a guardian of the forgotten, a token of a past that should never be ignored.

"In the heart of the night, where shadows meld with the darkened sky, the Black Bird dominates. Its eyes aglow pierce through the darkness. Its wings unfurl, vast enough to eclipse the moon, casting the world beneath into an impenetrable gloom. The bird's form is an aberration of the night. Each of its feathers, darker than oblivion, ripples with undeniable grace, absorbing all light and all hope. Its cry is a requiem for the desecrated land, a sonorous dirge that heralds the end of days. It is so profound that it vibrates through the reclaimed earth. The Black Bird's stare illuminates harrowing truths as it casts a verdict on humanity's follies.

"The Black Bird is not just a creature of flesh and feather. It embodies an ancient terror, a force that compels even the bravest hearts to cower in stupor. Its presence is a portent, a waking nightmare that cries of troubles yet to unfold.

"The legend speaks to the deep-seated fears and anxieties that such events can instill in the human psyche. According to lore, the Black Bird is a harbinger of doom and a manifestation of the land's suffering—a physical embodiment of the environmental

Similar Creatures in Folklore

Mothman

**POINT PLEASANT,
WEST VIRGINIA, UNITED STATES**

A cryptid with glowing red eyes and large wings, the Mothman was first sighted in the 1960s and is associated with impending disasters.

Thunderbird

NORTH AMERICAN INDIGENOUS FOLKLORE; ASSOCIATED WITH THE PACIFIC NORTHWEST REGION

A legendary creature in the form of a giant bird said to cause thunder and storms. It is revered and feared for its power and is said to protect humans from dark spirits.

Harpies

ANCIENT GREECE

Fearsome creatures with the lower body of a bird and the upper body of a woman, including the face. They are known as spirits of wind and destruction.

Alkonost

RUSSIA

A mythical creature with the head and face of a woman and the body of a bird, known for its enchanting melodies.

and emotional scars left by the Chernobyl disaster. It is said to have emerged from the collective consciousness of those affected by the tragedy, a dark mirror reflecting their anguish and despair. The Black Bird's role as an incarnation of the land's deepest fears is not just a metaphor but a profound truth—it is evidence of the power of myth and the human need to personify abstract concepts. In contrast, others see it as an ancient entity awakened by humanity's hubris and recklessness.

"In local folklore, daimones—spirits that wield power over natural forces—are common. The Black Bird fits this archetype. It is seen as an entity controlling the calamity, its wings beating in tandem with the chaos it sows. The Black Bird's presence is intertwined with destruction.

"The tale of the Black Bird serves as a cautionary reminder of the repercussions of human actions on nature. It is a mythic expression of ecological warning, urging respect for the delicate balance between human progress and environmental stewardship.

"As with many legends, the Black Bird of Chernobyl transcends its narrative to become a symbol of regret, warning, and the irreversible impact that specific events leave on both land and people.

"Such tales have long been prominent in human belief, warning of disaster long before it strikes. The likeness of this entity to the Mothman of distant lands is uncanny, suggesting a shared lineage in the annals of cryptid lore. In the throes of tragedy, the human psyche clamors for meaning amid chaos. It is a vivid reminder of your vulnerability and need for understanding in the face of what you do not know.

"O seeker of the veiled truths, in the quest to shield yourself from the Black Bird, let these distilled stratagems be your guide. Foster an aura of light within you, for darkness finds no purchase in the radiant heart. As twilight descends, invoke the guardian spirits or deities and beseech their protective embrace. Shun the dark arts, for they may draw the Black Bird's unwelcome scrutiny.

"As you surrender to slumber's call, cast a circle of protection, an unbroken barrier to safeguard your dreams. Arm yourself with resolve and the power of the old gods and stand firm against the darkness of the night.

"Attend the legend of the Black Bird, my friend, for within its narrative thrums the pulse of birth and ruin, the fragile equipoise of the wilds, and the earth's uncompromising vengeance. The Black Bird, often seen as a mark of destruction, is also a force of creation. A new life can emerge from the ashes of its wake, a paradox that adds complexity to the creature's nature and role in the narrative."

Remember the Silence before the Scream

APRIL 1986, CHERNOBYL, UKRAINE

Chernobyl was once a largely unknown town, its stories as unassuming as the gentle flow of the Pripyat River. But as 1986 waned, the darkness began to spread. Its wings cast long and dense shades over the city as it presaged a disaster of unprecedented scale. The workers, whose hands had built and tended the nuclear heart of the power plant, began to murmur of a sinister portent—the Black Bird of Chernobyl.

The protagonist of our story is Grigori Petrovich, a forbearing figure whose soul was inexplicably linked with the reactor's hum. As gray as the concrete walls surrounding him, Grigori's eyes had seen much, but he was ill-prepared for the ravager of ruin that would darken those skies.

The rumors began as fleeting wisps of smoke, glimpses of an entity flowing in and out of vision. Yet these sightings became more frequent as the days passed. The workers, with their voices hushed against the roar of the turbines, spoke of a vast and vile creature—a headless harbinger with wings that blotted out the stars and eyes that burned like lava from the fiery depths of hell.

Grigori, skeptical by nature, dismissed these tales as fanciful fears of the fatigued.

That is, until the night he saw it himself. The Black Bird was as real and tangible as the fear that gripped his heart. Its form was a blasphemy against creation, an affront to Mother Nature, a grotesque image silhouetted against the dark night sky. Its wings, with their immeasurable span, beat slowly and heavily with a tempo that sounded the death knell of a generation.

The creature's eyes found Grigori's. They were not merely red but a swirling maelstrom of crimson that seemed to pull at his soul. And where its head should sit, there was only darkness—a void that screeched of oblivion.

In the following days, Grigori was plagued by nightmares and visions of a world undone, a land poisoned and lifeless. He awoke each morning with the residue of the creature's scream in his ears—a clarion call that no one else could hear, a call that foretold the ruin to come.

When disaster struck on that fateful day of April 26, 1986, the Black Bird's dire prophecy was fulfilled. Once a behemoth of human achievement, the reactor became the epicenter of a catastrophe that would leave the land desolate, the air poisoned, and the name Chernobyl synonymous with mankind's hubris. The

64

explosion that tore through the night, the fire that burned with an unworldly fury, the invisible poison that spread its tendrils across the continent—all were foretold by the Black Bird's ominous presence.

As the world learned the name Chernobyl, Grigori knew that the Black Bird would forever be remembered in tandem with this place's legacy—a terrifying testament to the price of arrogance and a haunting reminder that some omens are the bearers of truth. Once a man of steel and steam, Grigori Petrovich now stood as a bystander to the end of an era. The Black Bird of Chernobyl was a herald of the apocalypse. Its augury cry was ignored and its prophecy was realized.

Grigori, however, would not live to see the full breadth of the aftermath. In the ensuing chaos, he vanished, leaving only whispers and a shadow that matched the Black Bird's own.

Echoes of Chernobyl: The Silent Resurgence of a Nuclear Ghost Town

Chernobyl is still one of the most radioactive places in the world. The town and the surrounding Chernobyl Exclusion Zone look like ghost towns today—the buildings are decayed and crumbled, and people are not allowed to live there. Even though it is radioactive, tourists used to visit the zone in large numbers. However, tourism has halted since February 2022, due to the Russian invasion of Ukraine.

The Exclusion Zone is under constant supervision by scientists and the area is still full of relics of its tragic past. Over a thousand natives refused to leave their homes even in the immediate aftermath of the disaster. Today, the zone is a testament to the resilience of nature, as wildlife has begun to thrive in the absence of human habitation.

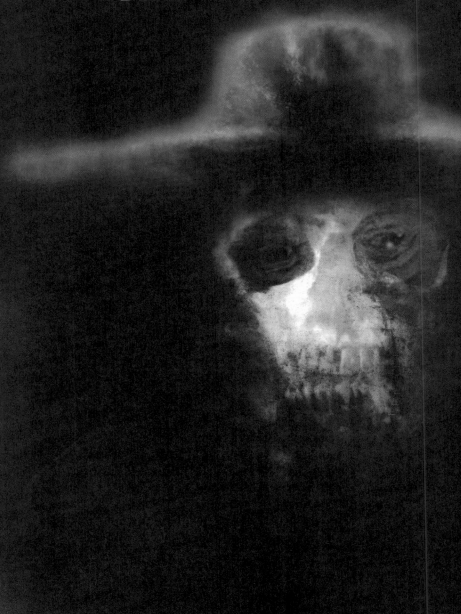

El Silbón's Haunting Tune

THE PALO SANTO TREE

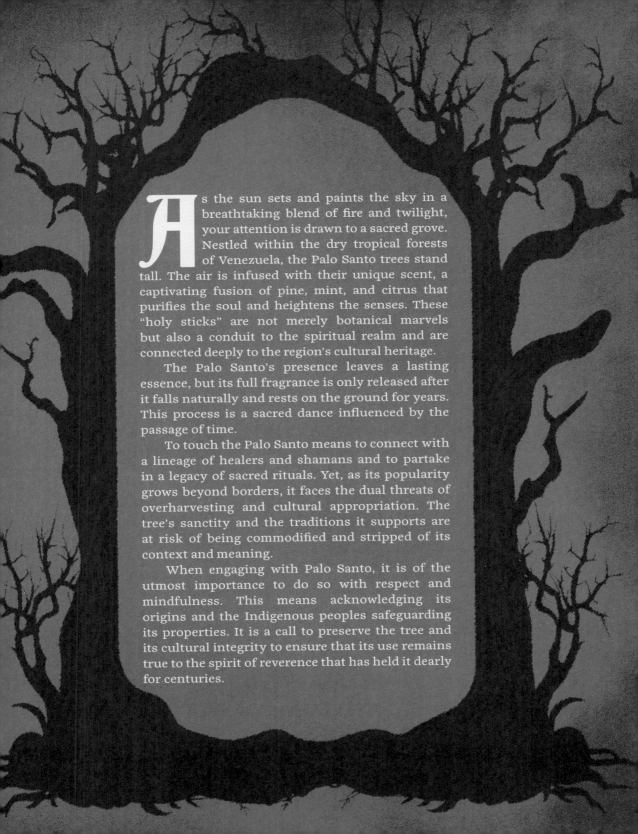

As the sun sets and paints the sky in a breathtaking blend of fire and twilight, your attention is drawn to a sacred grove. Nestled within the dry tropical forests of Venezuela, the Palo Santo trees stand tall. The air is infused with their unique scent, a captivating fusion of pine, mint, and citrus that purifies the soul and heightens the senses. These "holy sticks" are not merely botanical marvels but also a conduit to the spiritual realm and are connected deeply to the region's cultural heritage.

The Palo Santo's presence leaves a lasting essence, but its full fragrance is only released after it falls naturally and rests on the ground for years. This process is a sacred dance influenced by the passage of time.

To touch the Palo Santo means to connect with a lineage of healers and shamans and to partake in a legacy of sacred rituals. Yet, as its popularity grows beyond borders, it faces the dual threats of overharvesting and cultural appropriation. The tree's sanctity and the traditions it supports are at risk of being commodified and stripped of its context and meaning.

When engaging with Palo Santo, it is of the utmost importance to do so with respect and mindfulness. This means acknowledging its origins and the Indigenous peoples safeguarding its properties. It is a call to preserve the tree and its cultural integrity to ensure that its use remains true to the spirit of reverence that has held it dearly for centuries.

Y ou approach the holy wood cautiously, touching its trunk, still warm from the sun. As you close your eyes, inhaling deeply, a song full of sorrow and beauty floats toward you. The Palo Santo exhales, its voice a melancholic melody on the wind that speaks deeply to your soul.

"El Silbón," the tree sings, "is a tale of sin and retribution. Born from a heinous act of patricide, he is the cursed spirit of a man. He is a figure condemned to wander the earth with the remains of his victim in a sack on his back.

"El Silbón's legend is embedded in the cultures of Colombia and Venezuela, particularly in the Los Llanos region. It has evolved, intermingling with the peoples' fears and morals. Some believe he is a manifestation of the collective conscience, a warning against the dangers of unbridled desires and the consequences of one's actions.

"The name El Silbón translates in English to 'the Whistler,' a signature derived from his characteristic whistle that mimics the musical notes C, D, E, F, G, A, and B in descending and ascending order. This whistle is a musical signature of his presence, a spectral elegy that forewarns his approach.

"El Silbón's form is a ghastly sight—a gaunt figure towering above the grasses, his silhouette looming against the star-speckled sky. He carries a sack filled with the bones of his padre or, as some stories tell, the remains of his numerous victims. His features are those of a man starved not only of food but of mercy. His skin is racked taut over his skeletal frame. His eyes are sunken pits of despair that reflect the endless suffering of his soul.

"His behavior is as unpredictable as the wind that carries his foreboding whistle. He preys upon the wicked, particularly those who indulge in excesses of drink and flesh. Yet his presence is also a dark prophecy and a precursor to death to those who hear his mournful tune. In an unsettling dichotomy, it is said of his whistling that when it sounds close, he is far away; but when it seems distant, he is near.

"There are variations of this vision. Some accounts describe El Silbón as a towering figure moving through the treetops. In contrast, others depict him as an emaciated man with a hat that emphasizes his ghoulish and elusive nature. Regardless of the deviations, his whistle remains a constant and chilling element of his legend. He is an imprint of his deed, whistling an eternal sorrowful sonata that speaks of loss, love, and a moment's fateful choice. His ever-present whistle is a lamentation of his pain.

"El Silbón's backstory is grim, marked by violence and retribution. It begins with a young man, spoiled and used to getting what he wanted. His favorite meal was venison and he expected his father to provide it. However, when his father returned from a hunt without any deer, the son's anger erupted into a heinous act

Similar Creatures in Folklore

The Seven Whistlers
GREAT BRITAIN AND IRELAND

These mysterious birds, usually waders, fly together at night. Their eerie calls are considered a portent of impending doom. Coal miners in particular fear them.

La Lechuza (page 41)
MEXICO

La Lechuza is a witch capable of transforming into an owl or a large bird of prey. She whistles at night to lure unsuspecting victims, whom she snatches and carries away.

Fad Felen
WALES

Fad Felen has yellow eyes, teeth, and hair. Its deadly gaze kills anyone who sees it. It stalks its prey while whistling softly. It is the personification of the "yellow plague," a disease that ravaged Wales in the mid-sixth century.

Tunchi/El Tunche
AMAZON RAINFOREST

Tunchi is the malevolent spirit of a person who died in the woods. It protects the rainforest and whistles a particular melody. Responding to the sound invites Tunchi closer and may lead to a fatal encounter.

The Curupira
BRAZIL

The Curupira is a guardian of the forest. It has backward-facing feet to confuse hunters and emits whistles or bird-like calls to lead them astray. A protector of wildlife, it punishes those who harm the forest.

of patricide—he murdered his father in cold blood, removing the heart and liver as symbols of his rage."

The young man's grandfather, upon discovering the gruesome crime, was filled with wrath equal to the atrocity committed. He decided that mere imprisonment would not suffice for such a vile act. Instead, he subjected the boy to brutal punishment in the wilderness: He was tied to a post and whipped mercilessly, and alcohol, chili peppers, and lemon juice were then applied to the boy's wounds to intensify the suffering. As a final touch of torment, the grandfather placed a sack filled with the father's bones on the young man's back and unleashed two starving dogs on him. The grandfather then cursed him to wander with his father's remains forever.

"In another version of the story, El Silbón is driven not by uncontrolled rage but by a sense of betrayed justice. Upon discovering his father is having an affair with his daughter-in-law (El Silbón's wife), the young man is consumed by a mix of anger and despair. In an act of revenge, he kills his father. This desperate act sets him on a path of eternal wandering, burdened by the weight of his actions.

"All versions of El Silbón's tale are steeped in themes of familial betrayal and the consequences of one's actions. They serve as reminders that violence begets violence and that the repercussions of such deeds can last a lifetime—or, in El Silbón's case, an eternity.

"The folklore of El Silbón likely draws inspiration from the underlying principles found in spiritism, a belief system that acknowledges the existence of spirits and their capacity to interact with the living. In this context, El Silbón is depicted as a ghostly entity doomed to roam the earthly realm, carrying the weight of his past sins. The folklore reflects themes of redemption and communication with spirits.

"The landscape, particularly the sprawling Llanos (plains) of Colombia and Venezuela, influences these regions' folklore and spiritism practices. During the scorching summer months, Los Llanos experiences harsh droughts. The vast savanna becomes an otherworldly landscape with its dry grass and cracked earth. The parched land, shimmering heat, and lack of water create an eerie ambiance; inhabitants, fatigued by the relentless sun, may hallucinate or perceive unusual phenomena.

"In the face of El Silbón's mournful whistle, you, the vigilant traveler, must take up these time-honored defenses: First, hold a whip. Its sharp retort through the air is said to banish his advance. Next, bear chili peppers. Their fiery core is a bitter reminder of his cursed origins and repels his presence. Last, keep a faithful hound by your side. Its fervent barks are a sonic shield, reminding El Silbón of the starved dogs his grandfather set upon him. These wards are potent in the lore of the plains. May they grant you a measure of safety against the ghostly roamer.

"So, my friend, as you traverse these vast lands under the stars' watchful stare, remember the tale of El Silbón. He is the residue of past sins, the blackness that falls over the land, and a reminder that redemption is a path seldom walked by the damned. Take heed of my counsel, for in its wisdom lies your protection against the night's darkest melodies. Share your bread, guard your heart, be ever watchful, and let not the whistling of the grasslands lure you."

What Do You Want?

FEBRUARY 2024, CARACAS, VENEZUELA

Worn out from a long day's work, Miguel made his way home through the bustling avenues. The night was alive with the sounds of distant salsa music spilling from open windows, the murmur of voices bartering and bantering, and the occasional bark from packs of roaming street dogs, their forms darting between the pools of light cast by flickering streetlamps.

Yet beneath this thrum of urban life, there was an undercurrent of something else, something other. It was a noise that didn't belong. A soft whistle, barely perceptible at first.

Miguel paused. The more he attended to the sound, the more intelligible it became. It was a haunting melody that seemed both foreign and familiar, a tune that Miguel couldn't quite place but felt he'd heard before.

He resumed walking, quickening his step to outpace the sound that followed him. The whistle encircled him: now behind, now beside, as elusive as the breeze that stirred the litter in the gutters. Miguel couldn't shake the feeling that he was being watched.

A few nights later, he heard the faint whistle again, and as the months passed, the whistling became a sporadic companion during his nightly walks. Each time it drew nearer he quickened his pace. Nothing was ever there when he turned to look, always out of sight but unmistakably present.

Months later, alone on the streets of Caracas, the city's usual hum was muted, replaced by the distant sound of the Orinoco River brushing gently against its banks.

Then, cutting through the tension, the whistle returned. The sinister melody heralded an ancient and malevolent presence. Miguel felt a deep foreboding as the sound grew louder and more demanding.

Miguel's breath caught as he turned the corner, a narrow alleyway stretching before him. The moon hung low, elongated shadows writhing across the cobblestones. Miguel's pulse raced, and he pressed his back against the damp wall. His eyes darted left and right, seeking an escape. He wiped sweaty palms on his trousers, the fabric rough against his skin. And then, as if drawn by an invisible thread, he turned his gaze toward the darkest corner. There, half obscured by the night, stood a figure caressed in blackness. The Whistler leaned against the crumbling wall, features obscured by shadow. Miguel strained to see more detail, but the shades clung to the figure, unrelenting.

As if sensing Miguel's scrutiny, the Whistler moved to the edge of the shadows. His form emerged—a lean figure clad in tattered garments. His eyes remained hidden, but Miguel sensed their intensity.

Miguel's voice trembled. "Why are you following me?"

No answer.

And then, inexplicably, the Whistler stepped out fully into the moonlight. His face remained veiled, but his eyes—piercing and ageless—locked onto Miguel's.

Without warning, El Silbón then turned away. His steps echoed and Miguel followed. The alley widened, revealing the river's edge. Raindrops began to fall, mingling with the Whistler's melody.

"Wait!" Miguel called, but El Silbón paid no heed. His form blurred, merging with the night. Yet the whistle grew louder, overwhelming Miguel's senses until it drowned out the rain and his heartbeat.

He stood alone by the river, rain soaking his skin, but El Silbón's song lingered.

Nocturnal Melodies: The Global Taboo of Whistling in the Dark

Across many cultures, whistling after dark is considered a risky practice. For example, in North American Indigenous lore, the Blackfeet and Lakota Nations say that whistling at night calls upon spirits. Some tribes believe whistling at night can summon shape-shifters like the skinwalker or stikini.

In Korean culture, it is believed that whistling at night can call forth ghosts, demons, and even snakes. In Japan, whistling at night is believed to disrupt the peace and draw the attention of thieves and yōkai (a general term for a class of supernatural entities in Japanese folklore) known as tengu. Whistling at night is believed in Han Chinese culture to bring ghosts into the home.

The Tokoloshe's Curse

THE BAOBAB TREE

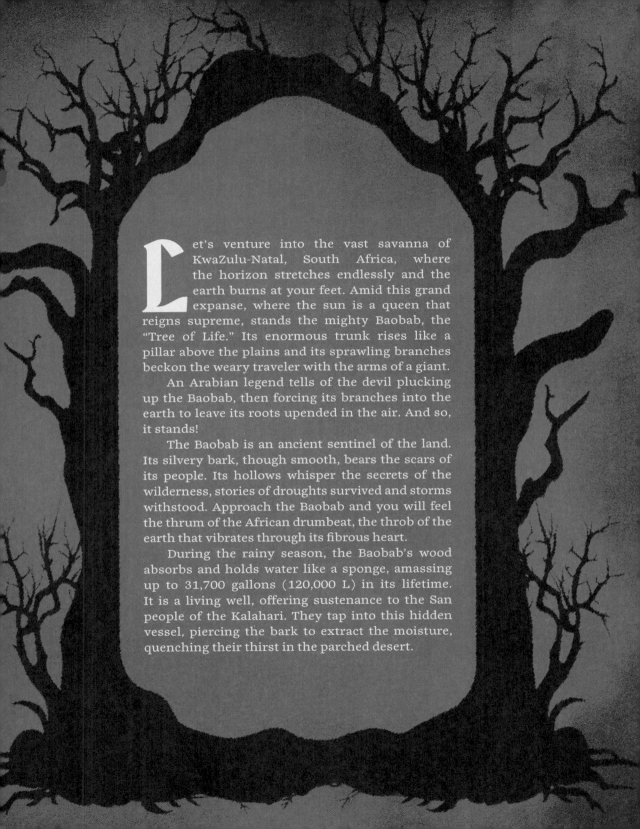

Let's venture into the vast savanna of KwaZulu-Natal, South Africa, where the horizon stretches endlessly and the earth burns at your feet. Amid this grand expanse, where the sun is a queen that reigns supreme, stands the mighty Baobab, the "Tree of Life." Its enormous trunk rises like a pillar above the plains and its sprawling branches beckon the weary traveler with the arms of a giant.

An Arabian legend tells of the devil plucking up the Baobab, then forcing its branches into the earth to leave its roots upended in the air. And so, it stands!

The Baobab is an ancient sentinel of the land. Its silvery bark, though smooth, bears the scars of its people. Its hollows whisper the secrets of the wilderness, stories of droughts survived and storms withstood. Approach the Baobab and you will feel the thrum of the African drumbeat, the throb of the earth that vibrates through its fibrous heart.

During the rainy season, the Baobab's wood absorbs and holds water like a sponge, amassing up to 31,700 gallons (120,000 L) in its lifetime. It is a living well, offering sustenance to the San people of the Kalahari. They tap into this hidden vessel, piercing the bark to extract the moisture, quenching their thirst in the parched desert.

Y ou sit beside the Baobab, its trunk wide and reassuring. As you trace the contours of its bark, a tiny chameleon catches your eye, its scales shimmering with a subtle dance of shifting hues. The Baobab senses your attention on the tiny creature and murmurs softly, "The Tokoloshe is born of water and shadow and is much like the chameleon. It is adept at disguise, elusive and fearful. It is a dwarf-like entity born from the darkest depths of lore, influenced by malevolent witchcraft to sow discord and bring harm.

"Rooted in the heart of Bantu mythology, the tale of the Tokoloshe spans the breadth of folklore. It is a legend infused with the spirit of the people, finding its place in the collective consciousness of various African cultures, primarily the Zulu. Known by many names—Tikoloshe and Thikolose—each reflects different African communities' unique cultural perspectives and traditions.

"Initially, the Tokoloshe was a water spirit known for its playful nature. It was associated with rivers and bringing laughter and joy to children. However, it evolved into a dreaded nighttime spirit when people mistakenly blamed it for mysterious deaths at night. These deaths were actually caused by carbon monoxide poisoning from fires in poorly ventilated homes. Yet the fear of the Tokoloshe grew from this misinterpretation, shifting its image from a benign sprite to a feared entity.

"In Bantu cultures, water spirits are often perceived as divine beings who inhabit water bodies such as rivers and lakes. They are honored for their crucial role in bringing life-giving rains or floods, which are essential for communities' sustenance. Rituals and offerings such as flowers, fruits, and incense are made to show gratitude and seek favor from water spirits.

"These aquatic entities are linked intimately with the initiation of healers. They provide enlightenment and insight, which they bestow upon select individuals. Water sources hold significant importance within the landscape, serving as sacred sites for performing ceremonies and facilitating interaction with the ethereal realm. Numerous African spiritual practitioners regard water as a sentient force, possessing the transformative capacity to shift one's condition, whether it be spiritual or corporeal. It wields the cleansing ability to protect against evil and the restorative power to transition one from sickness to wellness. Therefore, water is an indispensable component in many sacrosanct and curative rites.

"However, in the Tokoloshe's evolved form he is a being of nightmarish duality: both minuscule and monstrous, with a ghastly face that mocks his elfin form. His hide is a grotesque array of wrinkles and scales, reminiscent of an ancient reptile; his eyes, previously aglow with mischief, now gleam with a cunning light.

Similar Creatures in Folklore

Hobgoblin

ENGLAND

Hobgoblins are generally helpful household spirits, performing chores and bringing good luck to their hosts. However, they can be mischievous if offended.

Redcap

SCOTLAND AND ENGLAND

Redcaps are vicious and murderous goblins that inhabit old castles and towers along the Scottish border. They are named after their gruesome habit of dipping their caps in their victims' blood

Tengu (page 73)

JAPAN

Tengu are birdlike yōkai known for their martial arts skills and magical abilities. They can shape-shift into human or animal forms.

Dokkaebi

KOREA

Dokkaebi are horned goblins that create illusions and manipulate objects with their magic clubs. They are mischievous and unpredictable.

Knocker/Tommyknocker

UNITED KINGDOM AND
UNITED STATES

Knockers (also known as tommyknockers) are supernatural beings that inhabit mines. They will alert miners to imminent danger by knocking on the walls.

"His hands, though small, are dexterous and quick, adept at weaving threads of misfortune. Once the playful limbs of a water sprite, these hands now conjure spells of chaos, reaching out to meddle in mortal affairs. In some tales, the Tokoloshe also has one buttock and a penchant for females.

"This intricate creature has also evolved into a witch's familiar, its powers harnessed as an instrument of vengeance. In the dead of night, these witches, known as abathakathi, engage in dark rituals to awaken the Tokoloshe. With hushed incantations and the promise of a loved one's soul, they send it forth to settle scores and spread its evil.

"Furthermore, when colonial powers imposed their laws in Africa, they ignored local beliefs like the Tokoloshe. This led to a clash between African traditions and Western laws. The Tokoloshe's story evolved to symbolize this battle to preserve these customs, becoming an emblem of cultural conflict. This resistance was expressed through various forms of media. The Tokoloshe was depicted in art, literature, and film, often exploring themes of tradition versus modernity and serving as a social commentary. In the 2011 South African horror film *The Tokoloshe*, the creature takes center stage. The movie explores themes of urbanization, poverty, and cultural beliefs. The Tokoloshe becomes a metaphor for societal struggles, representing the clash between modern city life and traditional rural customs. In this way, the image of the Tokoloshe has helped to solidify its status as an insignia of indigenous resilience against foreign influence.

"Today, the Tokoloshe represents the importance of keeping African culture alive amid foreign influence and serves as a reminder of the dangers of ignoring traditions. It also warns against the negative emotions that can lead people to harm others.

"The Tokoloshe is more than a hushed legend of the past. It is a living and breathing part of folklore, especially in rural areas where the old ways are still revered. The creature's tale is told and retold as a story from bygone days and as a contemporary warning. This spectral presence continues to instill fear and caution, not merely in hushed tones around the fire but also in the everyday conversations of those who still believe.

"The Tokoloshe also manifests the fears that haunt the human psyche. It is a corporeal form of envy and hatred that festers in the hearts of those who turn to the dark arts. Zulu mythology often depicts it as a cautionary figure, a reminder of the consequences of greed and malice.

"To protect yourself from the Tokoloshe, you should raise your bed with bricks. This practice was born from the discovery that elevation could spare one from the threat of nocturnal asphyxiation, a practical solution wrapped in superstition's heavy wool cloak. You may also seek out the sangoma, a traditional healer among the Zulu people, to perform the ceremony known as umhlahlo. During these rites, you may discover the evildoer. Following this ancient wisdom can create a safety barrier against the Tokoloshe's mischief.

"As you wander the wilds of the night, my friend, heed this counsel and beware the Tokoloshe, the spirit of water and whimsy. Know that the wisdom of the ancients may be the very thing that keeps you safe from its tricksy talons."

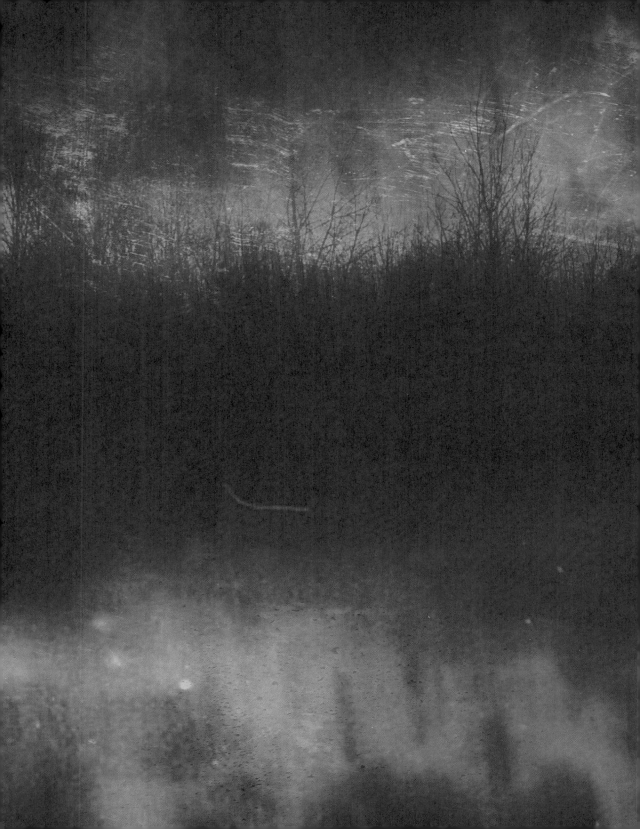

The Battle Had Begun

MARCH 2021, JOHANNESBURG, SOUTH AFRICA

Once a place of light and laughter, the house of the Dlamini sisters stood hollow, its darkened windows like empty eyes. Within, Emily and Rachael faced a supernatural enemy as archaic as the land itself—a Tokoloshe.

The creature had begun by revealing its presence subtly, moving a stone here or misplacing an object there. However, as time passed, its mischievous acts evolved into vicious ones.

On a moonless night, the true terror of the Tokoloshe was revealed. The sisters had been staying up for two weeks, listening to the guttural and grating sound that scraped across the roof. Emily was terrified, and Rachael clutched the blanket tighter and whispered her prayers, drowned out by the noise above.

The Tokoloshe's form was indiscernible, though its intention was palpable. The roof groaned under its weight and the tiles clattered like old bones.

With each passing moment, the Tokoloshe's antics grew bolder. Objects levitated and flung across rooms with a violent force. Water boiled without heat and coffee brewed for invisible guests.

Emily's heart pounded as she heard the Tokoloshe calling her name.

"*Emmmillly*," it hissed, the name stretching like a long-drawn bowstring, full of malice and dark delight. The creature tutted, a sound of disapproval and mockery as if chastizing Emily for her life choices.

"*Emmmillly*," the Tokoloshe called again, but this time, Emily was ready. She answered with a strength she did not know she possessed, her voice a clear, ringing bell in the night.

"We are not afraid of you!" she declared, and the Tokoloshe's laughter turned to a snarl of frustration. The battle had begun.

Rachael stood frozen in the dim light of the kitchen. The air was dense with the scent of lavender dishwashing liquid that should have been comforting. But comfort was a stranger in this house. It had been replaced by a creeping dread that slithered along the walls and settled in the pit of her stomach.

This night the Tokoloshe chose to reveal itself in a most personal and chilling manner. On the countertop, where the bottle of dishwashing liquid lay on its side, a message formed.

Rachael watched as the viscous liquid oozed slowly across the surface. It moved purposefully, guided by an unseen hand, spelling out her name in bold, dripping letters.

R-A-C-H-A-E-L.

Each letter was a taunt—a violation of her identity. The name on the counter seemed to pulse with a life of its own, and the letters writhed like rattlesnakes.

As the last of the liquid pooled at the end of her name, Rachael felt something shift within her. A primal instinct that had been long buried beneath the veneer of civilization rose to the surface.

The sisters sought the wisdom of the old ways. Salt lined their thresholds and chants filled the air.

On the fourteenth night, the Tokoloshe emerged. It was a creature of nightmares, its eyes hollow pits of despair, its body a twisted mockery of human form.

It stood at the foot of their beds, but Emily and Rachael did not falter. They met the Tokoloshe's gaze, their will a feral force that filled the room. The creature hissed from its mocking maw, a sound of ancient rage and eternal desire. But the sisters' resolve was more robust. With a final, ear-splitting shriek, the Tokoloshe vanished.

The Hopkinsville Encounter: A Glimpse into the Night of the Goblins

This infamous encounter, often called the Hopkinsville Goblin Case, involved a family who claimed to have been terrorized by a group of goblins in Hopkinsville, Kentucky, United States in 1955. The confrontation was prolonged and intense, sparking widespread fear. Those who saw them could only describe the goblins as hairless entities with pallid skin and distinguished by large, inky eyes and mouths devoid of lips. Their arms were disproportionately long and ended in hands that were either humanlike or webbed with protruding talons.

Grýla's Frightful Fable

THE ROWAN TREE

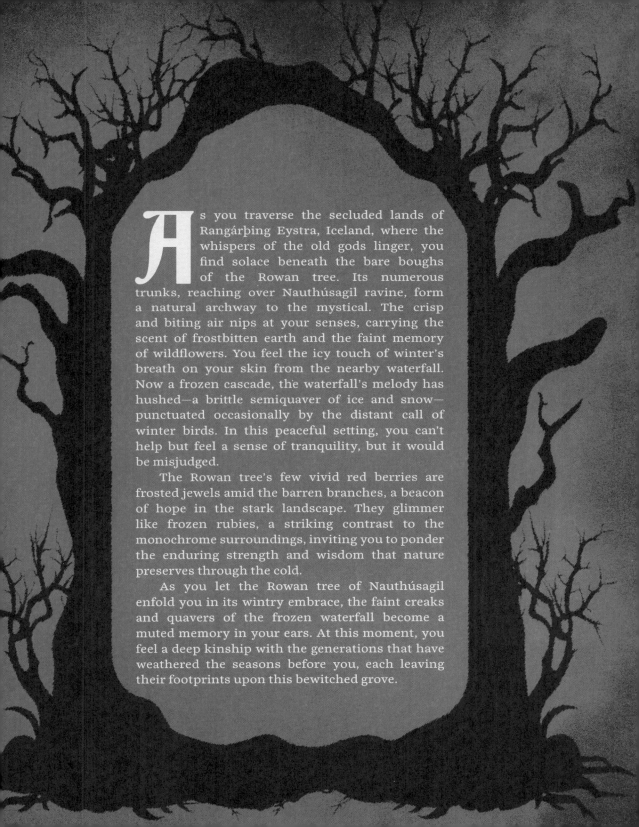

As you traverse the secluded lands of Rangárþing Eystra, Iceland, where the whispers of the old gods linger, you find solace beneath the bare boughs of the Rowan tree. Its numerous trunks, reaching over Nauthúsagil ravine, form a natural archway to the mystical. The crisp and biting air nips at your senses, carrying the scent of frostbitten earth and the faint memory of wildflowers. You feel the icy touch of winter's breath on your skin from the nearby waterfall. Now a frozen cascade, the waterfall's melody has hushed—a brittle semiquaver of ice and snow—punctuated occasionally by the distant call of winter birds. In this peaceful setting, you can't help but feel a sense of tranquility, but it would be misjudged.

The Rowan tree's few vivid red berries are frosted jewels amid the barren branches, a beacon of hope in the stark landscape. They glimmer like frozen rubies, a striking contrast to the monochrome surroundings, inviting you to ponder the enduring strength and wisdom that nature preserves through the cold.

As you let the Rowan tree of Nauthúsagil enfold you in its wintry embrace, the faint creaks and quavers of the frozen waterfall become a muted memory in your ears. At this moment, you feel a deep kinship with the generations that have weathered the seasons before you, each leaving their footprints upon this bewitched grove.

As you dangle your legs above Nauthúsagil, you find a comfortable position against the Rowan, feeling safe flanked by its many trunks. "The Yule Witch," the Rowan whispers, "is as timeless as the stones that line the stream's bed. She is the growler, the prowler, her voice a cavernous cacophony that makes even the bravest lose heart.

"In the dimly lit fissures of Icelandic lore lurks a figure so terrifying it epitomizes dread: Grýla, the Yule Witch. She is a giantess, the Archaic Mother, a troll of immense proportions. Her form rises from the mountains, a hulking, savage brute. She is the darkness that swallows the light, the winter that knows no end, a presence that instills a primal fear in the hearts of all who hear her groans.

"Her face is a grotesque configuration of horror, a sight that would freeze the blood of any who dare to look upon her: horns that spiral into the bleak sky, hooves that crush the earth beneath her weight, and a large, warty nose that sniffs the air for the sweet scent of fear. Her eyes are a pair of abyssal pits that gleam with a hunger that is never sated and her mouth is a cavern filled with teeth, blackened and sharp as the jagged ice of the glaciers.

"She has thirteen, or perhaps fifteen, tails, each writhing like leeches adorned with a hundred sacks. Within these sacks squirm unfortunate children, their screams a sweet harmony to her twisted soul. These are not just any children, but disobedient ones who have strayed from the path of purity and obedience. She stuffs these delinquent morsels into her mouth one by one. Their hollers are swallowed whole by her petulant, putrid mouth.

"Her beard is a matted tangle of grime and remnants of her ghastly banquets hang from her chin like woolly fringemoss. Her ears are long and drooping; they brush against her grotesque nose, listening for the wails of the naughty, the soundtrack of her eternal hunt.

"In the shadows of Grýla's fearsome legend lurk the Yule lads, her thirteen troublemaker sons. Each is a trickster in his own right, with names hinting at their very particular brands of naughtiness. From Spoon-Licker to Door-Slammer, they swoop down the mountains in the days before Christmas, each causing their own peculiar brand of chaos.

"Her husband, Leppaludi, is a lazy oaf, seldom seen and rarely remembered. He lounges in the cave, avoiding Grýla's wrath. Yet even he cannot dampen the spirits of the Yule Lads, who revel in their seasonal escapades.

"And then there's the Yule Cat, a beast as giant as a cottage, with eyes that gleam like the northern lights and claws sharp as icicles. This formidable feline prowls the snowy landscape, a purring predator seeking those without the gift of new clothes.

Similar Creatures in Folklore

Black Annis
ENGLAND

A hag with a blue face who is infamous for her iron claws and penchant for human flesh. She haunts Leicestershire's rural areas.

The Cailleach
SCOTLAND, IRELAND, AND ISLE OF MAN

She is often portrayed as a creator goddess, embodying the spirit of winter and the weather, an ancient divine hag.

Baba Yaga
SLAVIC FOLKLORE

A notorious witch who lives in a hut stilted on chicken legs. She is known for her cannibalistic tendencies and flying in a mortar, waving a pestle.

La Befana
ITALY

An ancient figure from Italian folklore, she emerges on the night of January 5 each year. La Befana leaves gifts in stockings—treats for the well-behaved and coal for the misbehaved.

Frau Perchta
ALPINE FOLKLORE

A witch-like being who emerges over the twelve days of Christmas. She is known to reward the good and punish the wicked, often in gruesome ways.

"The ogress Grýla, this witch of the north, is not a creature of flesh but of a nightmare. She symbolizes the primal terror that haunts the coldest, darkest nights. She is the Christmas Witch, the growler in the gloom. Her presence is a gruesome reminder of the darkness that can consume all. She is the night that swallows the light and the winter that knows no end.

"Her appetite is insatiable for the flesh of those who misbehave. She prowls the frozen tundra and seeks out the scent of rebelliousness. Her hooves leave no trace in the snow and her many tails flicker behind her like the feathers of a peacock.

"She is more than a witch. She is a force of nature, a blizzard of terror that sweeps through villages and snatches away the unruly to boil in her cauldron, a stew of retribution. Once spirited and defiant, her victims are reduced to mere tidbits for her supper, their lives extinguished and their families left alone to mourn their loss.

"Grýla epitomizes the need to explain the inexplicable and the mysterious disappearances that haunted the long winter nights. She is the personification of the land's harshness, a reminder of the dangers that lurk beyond the warmth of hearth and home.

"Grýla's folklore is interlaced deeply with the history and culture of Iceland. The country's stark, formidable environment, volcanic terrain, and long, dark winters conjure images of monstrous entities. The transition from paganism—with its horned gods and monstrous giantesses—to Christianity likely influenced her legend. Before the seventeenth century, Grýla was known to appear at any time, but as Christianity's influence grew, her appearances became explicitly associated with the Christmas season. This change reflects the integration of pagan elements into Christian traditions, where Grýla's role evolved to fit within the Christian narrative of Christmas. Her story has been passed down through generations, evolving while maintaining its horrifying essence and serving as a reminder of Iceland's ancient traditions and pagan roots.

"To protect oneself from Grýla, one must heed the old ways, the ancient rites that speak of purity and obedience. Keep the fires burning bright as a symbol of warmth and safety, letting the laughter of innocence fill the air and reminding you of the joy and innocence that can ward off evil. Holding fast to the bonds of family and community will provide sources of strength and protection. These are not just rituals but the keys to survival in the face of Grýla's gaze. Her watchful eyes pass over those who find strength in unity and who share the light of love and the warmth of kindness.

"Beware, for when the Yuletide draws near and the nights stretch long and cold, Grýla descends from her mountain lair. Be sure to listen to your parents and guardians—be kind, respectful, and do not stray too far from home, lest you find yourself within her grasp, another soul lost to the endless winter of her wrath.

"So, my dear companion, as you traverse the frozen paths of the land of ice, remember the tale of Grýla. She is the darkness of the winter solstice and the wail in the howling wind, a reminder that even in the season of giving, a shadow lurks waiting to be fed."

The Awakening

DECEMBER 2017, HÖFN, ICELAND

Jakob had run from his home in a rage, annoyed by all the relatives who had come to stay for the Christmas holidays, being nosy about Jakob's life and meddlesome about his future. The cause of his fury was trivial, he knew, but having run so far, he knew he had to find shelter quickly, as the cold was biting and unforgiving. Jakob turned his gaze toward the Skaftafell Ice Cave. Its crystal walls, formed by the mighty Vatnajökull ice cap, offered a refuge from the harsh elements and any prying eyes.

The silence embraced Jakob as he entered the Skaftafell, and he navigated through the serpentine passageways. Stalactites of ice adorned the ceiling like jagged chandeliers, while stalagmites rose from the floor to meet them in a frozen bite.

Finding a secluded alcove shielded from the cave's entrance, Jakob settled against the cold comfort of an ice column. He pulled his coat tighter around him, seeking its meager warmth as he lit his cigarette. The flame flickered, illuminating his face briefly and revealing a mix of youthful rebellion and vulnerability.

Suddenly, a subtle tremor disturbed the stillness of the cave, a faint vibration that grew steadily into a rumbling that resonated through the icy walls. Jakob's eyes widened with alarm as ice crystals trembled into life. He stubbed out his cigarette and stood up, his heart racing as he tried to make sense of what was happening. Was it the volcano Öræfajökull—or did something far more ancient and powerful stir within the depths?

Jakob dropped to the ground, breathing shallow and quick as he crawled toward the cavern's entrance and pressed his back against the cold wall. The cave continued to shudder, each vibration a thunderous warning of a presence outside.

Then, a new sound pierced the chaos—a deep, guttural sniffing that seemed to probe the air. Jakob's eyes were wide with fear as he realized something colossal was just beyond the ice wall, searching for him.

He dared not move as the sniffing grew louder, more insistent. The creature's voice was a low growl. "I can smell you, boy," the voice said. "The scent of your fear mingles with the smoke of your cigarettes."

The creature outside did not press further, happy to let the silence draw out between them. Then, in a voice as ancient as the land, the beast spoke. "Go home, boy."

With those parting words, the creature turned and walked away, its form gradually swallowed by the night as its steps faded into silence.

As its presence receded, Jakob gathered his courage. He knew he couldn't stay hidden forever. He peered out cautiously from the mouth of the cave.

The landscape was now serene, the snow untouched except for the massive trail through the snow leading up to Öræfajökull. Jakob followed the path with his eyes, tracing it as it wound its way toward the mountains.

On the cusp of where earth met the sky, he saw a figure retreating into the wilderness—the giant troll, Grýla, her form blending with the rocky outcrops.

In 2017, there was a significant increase in reports of missing children and young people in Iceland. In March alone, police in the capital area of Reykjavik received thirty-two requests for help in finding missing children and young people—a 53 percent rise on average compared to the previous two years. Coincidentally, during the same year, there was also increased activity from the Öræfajökull volcano.

The Miami Mirage: Alien Hoax or New Year's Pandemonium?

In 2024, an amateur video circulated online purportedly showing an alien at the Bayside Marketplace shopping center in Miami, Florida, United States. It depicted a figure at least eight feet (2 m) tall strolling outside the mall, leading to claims that aliens had landed on Earth.

On January 1, multiple 9-1-1 calls reported the sounds of what they thought were gunshots at the mall. In reality, a group of around fifty teenagers were shooting fireworks at people, causing panic and some looting. The situation escalated, prompting a citywide emergency declaration. The police arrested four teenagers involved in the disturbance. The video that went viral surfaced on New Year's Day.

As news of the video spread, it elicited a variety of reactions. While some were convinced of an impending alien invasion, others took to social media to express their skepticism, posting memes and questioning the authenticity of the footage.

The Yūrei's Sorrow

THE YOSHINO CEDAR TREE

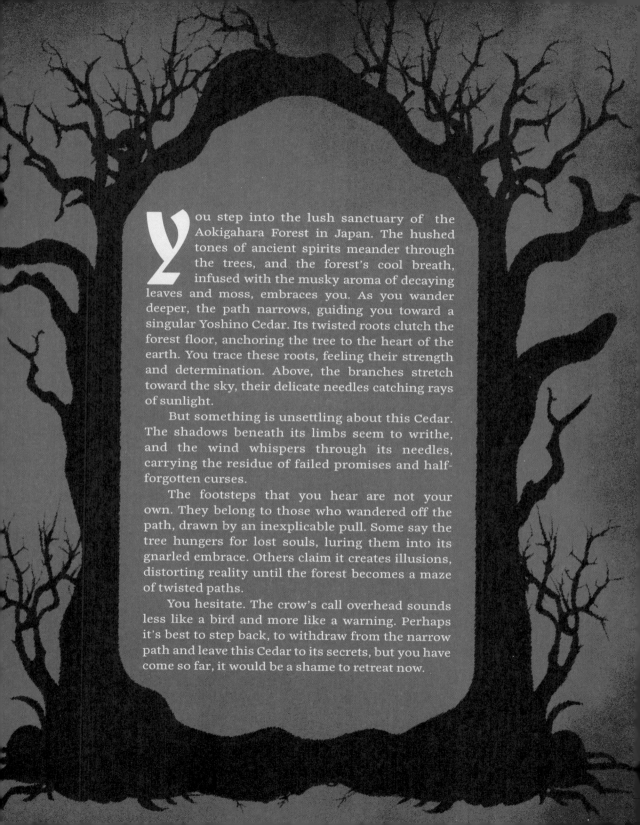

You step into the lush sanctuary of the Aokigahara Forest in Japan. The hushed tones of ancient spirits meander through the trees, and the forest's cool breath, infused with the musky aroma of decaying leaves and moss, embraces you. As you wander deeper, the path narrows, guiding you toward a singular Yoshino Cedar. Its twisted roots clutch the forest floor, anchoring the tree to the heart of the earth. You trace these roots, feeling their strength and determination. Above, the branches stretch toward the sky, their delicate needles catching rays of sunlight.

But something is unsettling about this Cedar. The shadows beneath its limbs seem to writhe, and the wind whispers through its needles, carrying the residue of failed promises and half-forgotten curses.

The footsteps that you hear are not your own. They belong to those who wandered off the path, drawn by an inexplicable pull. Some say the tree hungers for lost souls, luring them into its gnarled embrace. Others claim it creates illusions, distorting reality until the forest becomes a maze of twisted paths.

You hesitate. The crow's call overhead sounds less like a bird and more like a warning. Perhaps it's best to step back, to withdraw from the narrow path and leave this Cedar to its secrets, but you have come so far, it would be a shame to retreat now.

You perch upon a moss-covered boulder in the heart of Aokigahara, noticing that the forest floor is an amalgamation of shadows and whispers. Your eyes catch a subtle movement among them. A delicate firefly flits through the underbrush, its light a fleeting beacon in the encroaching dusk. "The Yūrei," the Cedar's voice rustles, "are akin to these brief sparks of life, dancing on the edge of sight. Their presence affirms the tales of old—heartache, retribution, and bonds that even death cannot sever."

The Cedar pauses as the firefly's glow fades and reappears, an invitation to delve deeper into the tales that linger in the gloom. "Conveyed deeply in Japan's spiritual and cultural heritage, the concept of Yūrei combines Shinto principles, Buddhism's wisdom, and local legends. It is a rich and subtle story that goes beyond only fear. Yūrei stories portray a worldview in which the living and the dead are intermingled in a shared existence and duty.

"According to Japanese beliefs, when a person dies, their reikon, translated to English as 'spirit,' leaves the body and enters a purgatory-like state. Proper funeral rites are essential for the spirit to reunite with its ancestors and become a defender to the family still living.

"However, if someone dies a brutal death, without the required funeral rites, or while possessing strong emotions (like revenge or sorrow), their spirit may metamorphose into a Yūrei. The Yūrei exist on earth until they can be laid to rest by completing absent rituals or resolving emotional conflicts that tie them to the physical plane.

"These spectral beings wander throughout Japanese lore, assuming many guises—from avengers of wrongs to guardians of the forlorn, from auguries of sorrow to watchers of the earthly domain.

"Yūrei are pale, translucent wraiths. Their forms are barely distinguishable from the creeping mists that slither along desolate moonlit paths. Their faces bear the marks of tragedy—eyes sunken into shadowed hollows, lips quivering, forever on the precipice of a scream that will never escape. White burial shrouds drape over their emaciated frames, while other Yūrei are shrouded in the decaying remnants of their mortal lives, garments now spectral and frayed. Their hair, as dark as the void itself, billows wildly, framing faces that embody anguish.

"They are nocturnal wanderers drawn to moonlit nights and the melancholic music of bamboo wind chimes. They glide through rice fields, their feet barely touching the dew-laden earth. Their hushed, mournful cries carry on the breeze, recounting their sorrows, seeking solace and closure.

"Be forewarned—their countenance is a treacherous tide that can turn in the blink of an eye. When the fires of vengeance ignite within Yūrei, their once sorrowful

Similar Creatures in Folklore

Gui
CHINA

Spirits of the dead that can be either benevolent or malevolent. Their nature depends on their death and treatment by the living. Some gui can cause harm, while others are worshipped as ancestors or deities.

Gwisin
KOREA

Spirits of the dead that remain in the world due to attachment, resentment, or unfinished business. Some gwisin seek vengeance, while others may be benign.

Phi
THAILAND

Spirits of the dead or supernatural beings that frequent the natural world. Phi can range from friendly or protective to hostile and dangerous.

features contort into nightmarish parodies of their former selves. Once sunken, their eyes blaze with a luminous light, a deathly glow that pierces you to burn deep into your core. Their hands, once human, now stretch out like the twisted limbs of ancient trees as if to grasp something just beyond reach.

"Woe betides any who cross their path.

"In the stillness of the night, their whispers speed through the air like a wind that carries the weight of unresolved anguish. Those who hear their cries are said to be marked, for Yūrei seek vessels—empty beings to appropriate and fill with their unresolved tales. The possession begins subtly, at first a mere flicker of a movement in your periphery and then a cold breath upon the nape of your neck. Then, as the Yūrei draws nearer, the air grows viscous with despair.

"Yūrei are bound by their tragic past. They are more than ghosts. They are the residue of intense emotions that resonate through time. Prisoners of their own stories, they seek to rewrite their endings through possession. Yet beware, for their touch is not a gentle caress but a desperate clutch, a drowning man's grip seeking salvation in the depths of another's soul.

"Their turmoil casts ripples of misfortune upon the living—bad luck, sickness, and suffering. Thus, ancestral veneration and the act of remembrance are sacred to ensuring serenity for both the domain of the living and that of the dead.

"Yūrei are forged by Japanese death lore and cultural consciousness, reflecting the societal contemplations of dying and the world beyond. They emerge in cautionary tales and parables connecting to the very heart of ancestor veneration. It was believed that the spirits of kin, if forsaken, could cause chaos in the living's daily existence.

"The Japanese honor their dead during the Obon festival by lighting lanterns to guide ancestral spirits back home. But what of those who remain lost? Yūrei denied these proper rites will linger. Their stories seep into Noh theatre, kabuki plays, and ghostly folk songs.

"For the intrepid traveler of the shrouded paths, carry talismans, amulets, and sacred seals to keep the haunting at bay. Engage in Buddhist rites, allowing sutras to be chanted and priests to conduct ceremonies of solace. These acts, steeped in tradition, may soothe the vengeful stirring of Yūrei. Share tales of these restless spirits, offering tokens of peace. In these gestures, you may grant them passage to the peace for which they yearn.

"Remember, these are not mere superstitions. Yūrei echo human longing. They are the embodiment of forgotten sorrows. Respect them, for they are one of the dark's most intimate secrets, the embodiment of collective grief and a reminder that death is not an end but a transition.

"Tread softly, dear wanderer. Should you feel the chill of their passing, offer a word of kindness, a gesture of understanding. For in the limbo of the Yūrei, compassion is the lantern that lights the path to repose. When the moon sits low and the wind carries whispers, Yūrei walk beside us.

Am I Dead?

MAY 2011, ISHINOMAKI, JAPAN

In the aftermath of the tsunami in the Tōhoku region of Japan, the streets of Ishinomaki were draped in an eerie stillness. During one of these somber nights, a local taxi driver, Kenji, encountered the inexplicable.

Kenji had been driving for hours. The radio crackled with the grave news of the tsunami's destruction, a constant reminder of the tragedy that had befallen the city. As he approached an intersection, a figure emerged from the mist—a woman, her clothes heavy with water and hair plastered to her pale face. She raised a hand. Kenji stopped his car.

The woman slid into the back seat and filled the cab with a chill that fogged the windows. "To the coast," she whispered, her voice barely discernable over the soft patter of rain. Despite the balmy weather, she wore a heavy winter coat, a contradiction that gave Kenji pause. Still, he nodded even as the hairs on his neck stood to attention.

As Kenji drove, the air grew colder with the scent of the sea and surf. The woman's reflection in the rearview mirror began to distort, her image trembling as if caught in a static haze of a malfunctioning screen. One moment, she was there; the next, she was nothing but a blur.

Kenji's knuckles paled as he clutched the wheel and the cab's interior flickered with an unearthly glow, the dashboard lights dimming and flaring erratically as if responding to the apparition's presence. The silence was oppressive, broken only by the distant crash of waves and intermittent sobs that emanated from the back seat—gut-wrenching wails that chilled the soul.

Suddenly, the radio crackled to life—a sizzle of static rising to a shrieking. Kenji flinched, his eyes darting to the mirror where the woman's face now appeared clear and yet not—her features flickering between human and something . . . else. Her mouth moved in a silent plea, or perhaps a curse, as the cab seemed to shudder in response to her anguish.

The world outside the windows warped, the streetlights stretching into elongated entities that streaked past in a blur. Kenji's reality shattered as the edges of his vision buzzed with an electrical terror that threatened to engulf him. He could feel her—the weight of her gaze, the heavy expectancy as if she wanted something from him.

As they neared the coast, the flickering intensified as a strobe of nightmarish images flashed before Kenji's eyes—visions of the tsunami's destruction and of lives snuffed out in an instant. The woman's last desperate moments as the sea claimed her. And then, with a final, guttural whisper that seemed to come from everywhere and nowhere, she uttered, "Am I dead?"

Then the cab plunged into darkness, the engine spluttered, and the world outside disappeared.

When the lights returned, Kenji was alone. The only evidence of his passenger was a lingering cold that refused to disperse, a damp mark on the seat . . . and a heavy winter coat folded neatly beside it.

The phenomenon of what was called the "tsunami ghosts" emerged in Ishinomaki, Japan, following the devastating tsunami that struck in 2011. Ishinomaki was one of the areas affected most severely by the waves. Encounters with tsunami ghosts refer to reported sightings or experiences of apparitions believed to be the spirits of those who perished during the disaster.

The Mystery of Okiku: The Living Locks of a Haunted Doll

The Okiku doll is a Japanese doll that is said to be haunted by the spirit of a girl who died of a fever. Her brother gave the doll to the girl, Okiku, in 1918. After the girl's death, the family noticed that the doll's hair, which was initially short, grew longer. They believed that the girl's soul had entered the doll. The family gave the doll to a temple in the prefecture of Hokkaido, where it is still kept and revered. The doll's hair continues to grow and is trimmed regularly by a priest. It is also purported to have supernatural abilities, such as changing facial expressions and moving by itself.

The Mystery of Changelings

THE HAZEL TREE

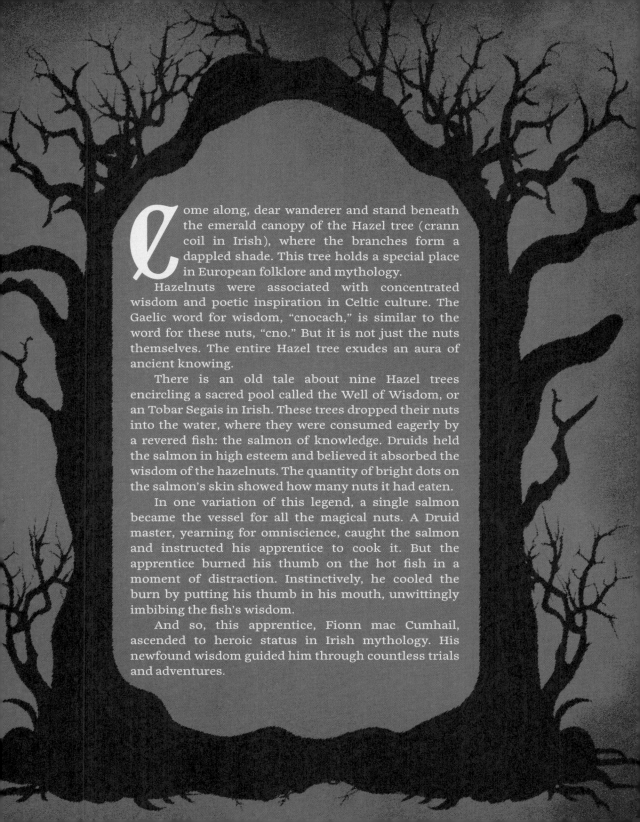

Come along, dear wanderer and stand beneath the emerald canopy of the Hazel tree (crann coil in Irish), where the branches form a dappled shade. This tree holds a special place in European folklore and mythology.

Hazelnuts were associated with concentrated wisdom and poetic inspiration in Celtic culture. The Gaelic word for wisdom, "cnocach," is similar to the word for these nuts, "cno." But it is not just the nuts themselves. The entire Hazel tree exudes an aura of ancient knowing.

There is an old tale about nine Hazel trees encircling a sacred pool called the Well of Wisdom, or an Tobar Segais in Irish. These trees dropped their nuts into the water, where they were consumed eagerly by a revered fish: the salmon of knowledge. Druids held the salmon in high esteem and believed it absorbed the wisdom of the hazelnuts. The quantity of bright dots on the salmon's skin showed how many nuts it had eaten.

In one variation of this legend, a single salmon became the vessel for all the magical nuts. A Druid master, yearning for omniscience, caught the salmon and instructed his apprentice to cook it. But the apprentice burned his thumb on the hot fish in a moment of distraction. Instinctively, he cooled the burn by putting his thumb in his mouth, unwittingly imbibing the fish's wisdom.

And so, this apprentice, Fionn mac Cumhail, ascended to heroic status in Irish mythology. His newfound wisdom guided him through countless trials and adventures.

As you consider the Hazel's history, your eyes are drawn to a subtle rustling among its branches. It is not the wind but a small, industrious squirrel. Its sharp claws, with awe-inspiring agility, climb and navigate the bark. Its eyes gleam with intent as it scurries after the Hazel's prized nuts. The tree, amused by the creature's antics, shares a hushed chuckle. "The Changeling," it suggests, "is akin to this squirrel, ever searching and stealing. They are not only replacements for human young but pursuers of human's hidden bounty. They remind us that a keen sight is our finest ally in pursuing truth.

"The mythology of Changelings is entrenched deeply in European folklore, particularly within ancient Celtic and Germanic cultures. These tales often describe Changelings as the offspring of fairies or elves, who were believed to swap their own weak or deformed children with healthy human infants. This exchange was thought to either strengthen the fairy stock or allow the elders to live the remainder of their lives being cared for by humans—or even use the abducted mortal children as an offering to the devil.

"The belief in Changelings was widespread across Europe, with variations of the lore appearing in different regions. For instance, it was not uncommon for fairies to take adults in Ireland and Scandinavia.

"Changelings emerge from the twilight, born of magic and mischief. Their legacy is an ensemble of Fae trickery and human stories. They often resemble the human child they replace, yet subtle distinctions mark them as different. Their eyes hint at their true nature, whether displaying wisdom beyond their years or an insatiable hunger. Their unworldly whims create a sticky web of confusion and chaos.

"The Changeling wears a mask of, well, otherness—a face that mimics humanity but never quite fits. Its skin, as if fashioned from moonbeams, is translucent, revealing veins like silver threads. Its eyes, large and luminous, hold secrets older than time itself and peer out from hollow sockets, seeking warmth and yearning for human connection.

"Its limbs are fragile and brittle, yet the Changeling moves with a transcendental grace, gliding through moonlit glades and leaving no trace upon the mossy earth. Fingers, elongated and delicate, reach for forgotten memories—those stolen from the babe it replaced.

"When it speaks, the Changeling's voice carries the residue of distant kingdoms. Both entranced and unnerved, villagers listen, for the Changeling's speech holds the weight of forgotten lullabies and half-remembered dreams.

Similar Creatures in Folklore

Oaf

ENGLAND

A Changeling child left by elves, historically believed to be clumsy or awkward.

Wechselbalg/Wechselkind

GERMANY

These terms refer to a fairy child exchanged with a human infant. The wechselbalg is often depicted as unable to grow or develop normally and may exhibit strange behaviors or have an insatiable appetite.

Bortbyting

SCANDINAVIA

In Norwegian mythology, this term refers to a troll's infant exchanged for a human baby. These Changelings are often difficult to please and have a voracious hunger. In Swedish folklore, stories of Changelings may be connected to stories of elves and other supernatural beings. Swedish bortbytings are often described as having an unusual appearance and behavior.

Plentyn Newid

WALES

This Welsh term for a Changeling describes a fairy youngster who has replaced a human child. These children are said to bring bad luck and are often recognized by their constant crying and odd features.

Dziwozona

POLAND

Dziwożona is often depicted as a malicious entity that replaces human infants with her own offspring to be raised by humans.

Tàcharan

SCOTLAND

Like other Changelings, Scottish tàcharans often possess voracious appetites. Stories also recount that tàcharans look like the stolen child, but act much older in behavior (like drinking whisky or playing the bagpipes), betraying their true nature. To avoid a human child being replaced with a tàcharan, one common piece of advice is to place a horseshoe outside the front door of the house.

"The Changeling feeds on emotions—the raw quintessence of human experience. It craves laughter and tears. When a mother weeps for her lost child, the Changeling absorbs her sorrow into its own fractured soul. Yet its deep ache and longing can never be filled—it remains insatiable and forever seeks more.

"Look closely at the babe in the cradle—the one who refuses to suckle, whose eyes hold ancient wisdom. Observe the child who dances alone in the moonlight, its laughter is a haunting chuckle. Every Changeling bears a bargain struck in the starless sky—a stolen life exchanged for a stolen soul.

"And what of redemption? Can a Changeling break free from its Fae bonds? Some say love holds the key—the touch of a mortal hand and a mother's embrace. But such redemption is rare and elusive. The barrier between worlds grows stronger and the Changeling remains trapped, forever yearning for what it can never truly understand.

"The lore of the Changeling is also a flame of warning to all parents, a tale told by the fireside to instill vigilance. It speaks to the primal fear that grips the heart of every caregiver—the dread of losing one's offspring to the spirits of the fairy world. In the face of the unexplainable, it is a myth that offers a semblance of solace, a way for a community to make sense of the bewildering afflictions that may befall their young. Changeling stories reflect the fears and beliefs of these cultures, often serving as explanations for the unexplained and as a warning to protect the vulnerable from malevolent forces.

"In this ancient story, the Changeling stands as a metaphor for the inexplicable, a bridge between the tangible and the mystical, and a reminder of the eternal watchfulness required to protect the innocence of the young from the enchanting yet perilous embrace of the Fae.

"In the shadowed corners of these age-old tales, there lies a more somber truth, a reflection of the hardships faced by those in the mortal realm. Changeling lore also served as a poignant explanation for the families of children born with disabilities or who fell ill in times when such occurrences were poorly understood.

"In the dim light of a peat-fire hearth, a mother cradles her child, once vibrant and full of life, now listless and distant. Whispers of a Changeling's presence begin to stir among the villagers. It is said that the Fae took the ailing youngster, leaving one of their own in its stead. It speaks to the heart's yearning for a reason amid the cruel caprices of fate.

"Changelings are treated with awe and trepidation in their guise as the afflicted children. They are cared for, yet watched with a wary eye, for the parents grieve not only the loss of their child but also the arrival of an enchanted being. With its unearthly quirks and unfathomable ailments, the Fae child becomes both a burden and a blessing.

"Changelings symbolize the challenges faced by those who are different. They embody the community's struggle to accept what it cannot understand and the compassion that arises when it is faced with these challenges.

"Guardian of the fireside, in the whispered tales of old Europe, Changelings are spoken of with hushed tones. To safeguard the innocent from such stealthy exchanges, heed these time-tested counsels: Never let the young out of sight, especially near the haunts of the Fair Folk such as forests, groves, mountains, waterfalls, and in particular rings of mushrooms (also known as fairy rings). Tend to your home carefully, as cleanliness is a weapon against fickle spirits.

"In the lore of the ancients, rituals of protection were observed with reverence. Lay fireside tongs across the cradle, for iron is anathema to fairy kind. Adorn the cradle with red garments, a color of power and portent and a ward against the Fae. Suspend crucifixes above sleeping babies, for such symbols are as lullabies to such forces. Anoint the young with holy water, invoking the divine shield against the mischievous and the malevolent.

"Let these practices be your wards, guardian of the hearth, and may the peace of your home be unbroken by the Fae's subtle hand.

"Heed well these tales, my dear confidant, for Changelings are more than a myth. They embody the unknown and are heralds of change. They challenge us to look beyond, to question and learn. May you tread carefully in moonlit groves and if ever you encounter a Changeling, offer it a kind word. For beneath its borrowed guise lies a heartache older than time—a longing for belonging and a hunger for home."

Come and Play?

JULY 2005, BRISTOL, ENGLAND

Young Maisey gazed through the rear window of her home in Bristol. The garden, a menagerie of grasses and concealed truths, unfurled before her. And there, bathed in the moon's early evening glow, stood the dwarf. He was a mystery wrapped in a three-foot (1 m) frame, just waiting to be solved. Maisey's heart quickened and her breath caught in her throat as she realized she was about to begin a journey she could never have imagined.

This was no fairytale sprite, no cherubic gnome. His face bore the consequence of his years, wrinkled by forgotten miseries. Snow White's kin, perhaps, but his features were twisted by time.

Maisey was a girl of ten summers, and her life was a blending of ordinary days and simple joys. Her home was a quaint farmhouse nestled between the embrace of ancient oaks and rustling rows of corn.

The yard was Maisey's kingdom, where her imagination turned tall grasses into forests and the garden pond into an ocean teeming with sea monsters. She was familiar with every nook and cranny of her home. Yet the appearance of the dwarf had unearthed a new layer to this familiar landscape.

The dwarf, with his ancient eyes and cryptic smile, seemed to have stepped out of one of Maisey's beloved books, offering an adventure that was impossible to resist.

But Maisey was also wise beyond her years, a trait gifted by her mother, who told stories of the fairies. She taught Maisey to be cautious, to see beyond the surface and to look for the truth.

The dwarf approached the window with a beckoning gesture, an invitation proffered with moonbeams. His weathered and insistent fingers traced intricate patterns on the glass. "Come," he murmured. "Come and play."

Maisey's fingertips brushed against the surface of the window, torn between fear and an insatiable curiosity.

Maisey's heart raced like a deer at the forest's edge, enticed by the lush meadow beyond, but with eyes alert and cautious of a hidden predator. She unlocked the door with a trembling hand and stepped outside. The dwarf led her along a path invisible yet irresistible.

"Follow," the dwarf whispered, and the choice was a ribbon of destiny that shimmered in the air. To step forward was to unravel the fabric of reality, to surrender to the unknown. But Maisey was no fool. A cold and gripping fear wrapped around her and she retraced her steps hurriedly.

That night, she would not be ensnared. The dwarf's face crumbled; an ancient anger shown in his wrinkles. He watched, his eyes filled with disappointment, as Maisey darted back to the safety of her home.

The dwarf, one of the Fair Folk, had been denied. As Maisey retreated, his visage began a grotesque transformation. His eyes now flickered with an evil fire. The wrinkles on his face deepened and contorted into a snarl of fury and suffering. His mouth, which had whispered promises of otherworldly adventures, now twisted into a scream of thwarted desire. The air around him grew thick with the scent of mildew and rot, and the ground where he stood seemed to wither and die.

His true self revealed, he was a creature of reckoning and retribution. He vanished into the night with a muttered promise to return.

The Mên-an-Tol: Stones of Legend and Lore

In Cornwall, England, there is a small formation of ancient standing stones called Mên-an-Tol. In Cornish, Mên-an-Tol means "the stone of the hole," and it's also referred to colloquially as the Crick Stone. Three upright granite stones make up the formation: two standing stones on either side and a round stone with a hole in the middle.

The Mên-an-Tol is believed to have originated in either the late Neolithic period or the early Bronze Age. It is possible that the location was originally a part of a stone circle, or a chamber tomb used in fertility rites. There is also conjecture that the holed stone was a natural occurrence rather than a sculpture created purposefully.

According to legend, a woman had a son who was sickly and weak. She suspected he was a Changeling left by fairies. She consulted a wise man, who told her to take the boy to the Mên-an-Tol at midnight and pass him nine times through the hole in the middle stone. She did as instructed. As she passed the boy through the hole for the ninth time, she heard a loud scream from the other side. She saw her real son, healthy and strong, running toward her. The Changeling had vanished, and the fairies had returned her child.

The Wild Hunt's Pursuit

THE APPLE TREE

Y ou stray into the dappled sunlight of an orchard, where the fragrance is syrupy with the sweet scent of ripening fruit. There before you stands the Apple tree, a vessel of abundance, its branches heavy with blushed fruit just within your reach. The leaves are caressed by a gentle breeze that whispers of ancient tales and timeless rituals.

This tree symbolizes knowledge and immortality and is prevalent in English legends of old. The Apple tree is not just a sacred portal but a mystical gateway to other worlds where gods and mortals mingle in a dance of infinite wisdom.

As autumn's warm glow envelops the orchard, the Apple tree is a beacon of festivity, its bounty celebrated in joyous harvest festivals. The Celts revered it in their Samhain festivities, believing you could touch the otherworld beneath its boughs. It was a time of divination, where apples became conduits of prophecy, revealing fates and fortunes with every slice and pip, adding to the season's merriment.

In the heart of winter, as the new year dawns, the Apple tree symbolizes communal tradition and hope. January marks the time for the archaic custom of wassailing, a ritual steeped in pagan roots.

It is a time of merrymaking and magic, where the community joins under the largest Apple tree to awaken the slumbering trees with shouts of "Wassail!" amid the clamor of pots and pans to drive away any malevolent spirits, creating a sense of unity and fruitful hopes for the future.

Y ou press your spine against the tree's sturdy trunk and reach out to clasp its decadent bounty. The Apple tree is hardy and enduring and it rustles its leaves in a hushed tone, mourning the disconnect between your world and the mystical. Its voice is as tart as its fruit and cuts through the stillness. "The Wild Hunt," the tree intones, "is not just a myth. It manifests nature's wildness and the untamed spirit that runs through everything.

"In the ancient groves of Europe, the legend of the Wild Hunt roars to life. It is a tale as old as the forests, a spectral parade that rides with the storm's fury and the snow's silence.

"The Wild Hunt is a phantasmal chase led by gods or ghosts. It is a motif that has seeped into the soil of many a European culture. They accompany a majestic and menacing figure, a spectral leader whose presence commands the night. This procession of spirits can sweep across the sky as silent as the grave, or race along forgotten roads with the roar of thunder. Their passage is marked by a deep chill that burrows into the bones or a thunderous clamor that stutters one's soul.

"Sometimes, elves and fairies join the ghostly throng, adding an ethereal glow to the cavalcade. The howling wind can also carry the sounds of otherworldly hounds, their barks reverberating through the cold air, while carrion birds circle overhead, casting ominous shadows upon the ground.

"The appearance of this phantasmal host is a harbinger of change, a portent of catastrophes yet to unfold. It is said that where the Wild Hunt rides, plagues, wars, and famines follow, and those who lay eyes upon this spectacle may find their fates intertwined with these misfortunes. The Hunt is a reminder of the ancient bond between humanity and the mystic forces that govern life and death.

"Some believed that peoples' spirits could be drawn away in their sleep to join the ghostly march and those who come upon the Hunt might be snatched to the underworld or the fairy kingdom.

"The Wild Hunt is an enduring legend, an emblem that captures your primal fear of what lies beyond death and darkness. The motif of the Wild Hunt was formed through a combination of ancient and medieval beliefs in nocturnal processions of spirits. These notions were coined in the early nineteenth century under the phrase 'wild hunt' by famed German author Jacob Grimm. The label has since been used to represent supernatural forces, often associated with omens, changes, or transitions.

"The myth of the Wild Hunt is believed to have originated from an ancient pagan belief in a nighttime ride of the valiant dead, guided by a fertility and death-related god like the Anglo-Saxon Woden, Germanic Wotan, or Norse Odin. This divine figure was often accompanied by a consort, a fertility goddess.

Similar Creatures in Folklore

Furious Host
EUROPEAN FOLKLORE

A spectral group often led by a legendary figure, sometimes associated with storms and chaos, believed to be souls in purgatory or a punishment for sinners.

Oskoreia
SCANDINAVIA

A ghostly hunt led by Odin, characterized by its eerie silence and the potential to bring misfortune or death to those who witness it.

Fairy Cavalcade
IRELAND

A parade of fairies, sometimes joined by the dead, that can enchant humans into joining them, often resulting in the loss of time or memory.

Herod's Hunt
BRITISH FOLKLORE

A British variation of the Wild Hunt said to foretell disaster or death, with spectral hounds known for their relentless pursuit of sinners' souls.

Gabriel's Hounds
NORTHERN ENGLAND

Phantom dogs whose eerie howling is an omen of death, believed to be the souls of unbaptized children wandering the earth.

"In turn, these archaic beliefs may have been influenced by the natural world, where the fury of storms and the quiet of snowfall could be integrated easily into tales of spirits riding through the night. The Wild Hunt, therefore, may roar to life with the storm's fury, embodying the raw power of nature, or glide with the snow's silence, a spectral presence as serene as it is ominous.

"This connection to weather in pre-Christian times is emblematic of how ancient peoples interpreted their environment and its phenomena through myth. It was a way to make sense of the world around them—where gods and spirits were as real as the wind and rain—and it endures as a homage to your forebears' mystic bond with the cosmos.

"Christian interpretations of the Wild Hunt varied but were often revised into a Christian context to fit new narratives. In some cases, it was demonized as a procession of damned souls or witches, reflecting Christian views on paganism and heresy. In other instances, it was assimilated into Christian folklore, with figures like Saint Hubert or Saint Eustace taking on roles similar to pagan leaders of the Hunt.

"Hearken, O wayfarer of the elder paths! When the night is rife with the Wild Hunt's call and the sky thrums with the thunder of spectral hooves, take these ancient advisories to heart: Seek the shelter of hallowed ground, for the Hunt shuns the sanctified. Carry an oak leaf within your pocket, plucked on All Hallows' Eve, as a token of nature's dominion to stop the host's pursuit. If caught in their path, lie prone upon the earth, blend with the soil you came from, and let the Hunt pass overhead.

"Should the hunters lock eyes with you, offer a tithe to the wilds—a measure of grain or a drop of spirits—for the old ones favor the generous. Let these wards be your guard, traveler of the twilight, and may the fury of the Hunt pass you by."

Riders of the Storm

FEBRUARY 1977, HEREFORD, ENGLAND

Little Willow, a mere wisp of a child at four winters, stood barefoot upon the dew-smattered grass in her family's garden, her gaze lifted to the tumultuous heavens. The wind was a foreboding precursor of the tempest to come as it swept through the elms.

Her eyes, vast vats brimming with untainted wonder, latched onto a spectacle and her breath caught in her throat as she watched a phantasmal cavalcade traverse the skies. The Wild Hunt that stretched across the diurnal expanse was a reverberation from an era when deities and mortals trod the same hallowed ground. Its ranks were composed of figures cloaked in the majesty of oblivion. Their mounts were forged from the spirits of storms and they expelled breaths of cosmic dust.

At the vanguard of this spectral legion was their chieftain, a figure carved from the darkness itself, his cloak a fluttering banner of obscurity. With every gust of wind, his horn sounded a clarion call through the air, reverberating deep into the earth's bones.

As the storm gathered and cast its devilish shadow over the day, the Wild Hunt's pace grew in intensity. The leader's horn was now a glowing beacon amid the growing gloom, summoning forth the spirits of the air. His followers answered in kind with a cacophony of spectral cries. Each flash of lightning was their lance, each rumble of thunder their drumbeat.

Suddenly, the procession halted and the air grew viscous. The riders turned their gaze earthward, their eyes glowing with an empty light that tore holes through reality.

The leading rider, a figure of towering darkness atop his spectral steed, raised his arm deliberately, his finger extended toward the young girl. Caught in his ghostly stare, Willow felt a chill deeper than the winter's frost seep deep into her being. His eyes were blacker than the abyss itself. Within their depths swirled forgotten nightmares, memories of blood-soaked battlefields, of a world destroyed, and the anguished cries of lost souls. As his dead stare fixed upon Willow, he hungered not for flesh or bone, but for something more primal. Perhaps he understood that humans, in their folly, were destroying the very earth that birthed them and that the Wild Hunt would race no more.

Her mother, Debbie, had been amid her daily chores when she felt an inexplicable urge to check on her daughter. In the tempest-tossed garden stood Willow, a fragile child against the fierce dance of the heavens.

The skies above roared with a fury that spoke of ancient battles and timeless chases. Debbie's heart pounded like a drum in the grip of the storm. She dropped the dishcloth she had been using, forgotten, and ran without a second thought. Her feet carried her across the threshold, through the door, and into the garden, where the wind whipped her hair and raindrops splattered against her face.

"Willow!" she screamed, but it was barely a whisper over the clamor of the elements. She reached out and enveloped her daughter in a tight embrace. Willow turned, her eyes wide, and in that moment, Debbie knew—something of another world had shown itself to her child. "Willow, love, what do you see?" she asked, her voice just heard over the clamor of the elements.

"Mummy, the riders," Willow said, her tiny hand pointing to the heavens. "They fly in the sky."

The Ghostly Santa Compaña: A March of Doom

The Santa Compaña is a haunting legend from the Iberian Peninsula of southwestern Europe, particularly Spain and Northern Portugal, telling of a ghostly nocturnal procession. Legend states that the group is led by a living person, unwittingly cursed to bear either a cross or a cauldron of holy water through the night, with no memory of the ordeal come morning. This curse can only be lifted by passing the burden to another, who then becomes the new leader of the spectral parade. The souls that follow are invisible, yet their presence is betrayed by the scent of melting wax, the whisper of their movement, or the eerie sounds of their moans, prayers, and tolling bells.

Considered an ill omen, the Santa Compaña is said to foretell death, illness, or other misfortunes to those who see it or intersect its path. To evade this curse, one must perform protective rituals, such as lying prostrate on the ground, drawing a circle with a cross inside, or uttering prayers or incantations.

The Pontianak's Scent

THE FRANGIPANI TREE

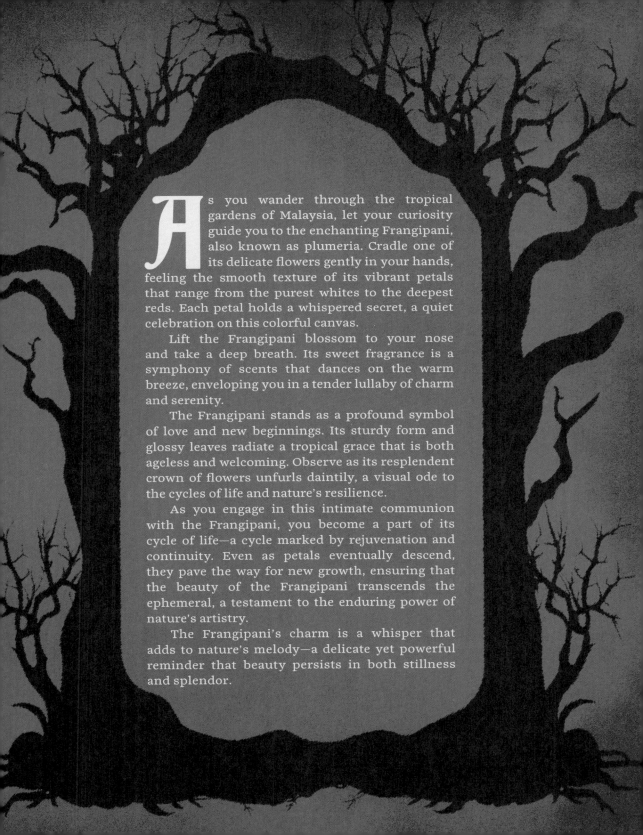

As you wander through the tropical gardens of Malaysia, let your curiosity guide you to the enchanting Frangipani, also known as plumeria. Cradle one of its delicate flowers gently in your hands, feeling the smooth texture of its vibrant petals that range from the purest whites to the deepest reds. Each petal holds a whispered secret, a quiet celebration on this colorful canvas.

Lift the Frangipani blossom to your nose and take a deep breath. Its sweet fragrance is a symphony of scents that dances on the warm breeze, enveloping you in a tender lullaby of charm and serenity.

The Frangipani stands as a profound symbol of love and new beginnings. Its sturdy form and glossy leaves radiate a tropical grace that is both ageless and welcoming. Observe as its resplendent crown of flowers unfurls daintily, a visual ode to the cycles of life and nature's resilience.

As you engage in this intimate communion with the Frangipani, you become a part of its cycle of life—a cycle marked by rejuvenation and continuity. Even as petals eventually descend, they pave the way for new growth, ensuring that the beauty of the Frangipani transcends the ephemeral, a testament to the enduring power of nature's artistry.

The Frangipani's charm is a whisper that adds to nature's melody—a delicate yet powerful reminder that beauty persists in both stillness and splendor.

Y̶ou crouch beside the blooming Frangipani. Its sweet, enchanting scent drifts gently to you, a comforting and alluring fragrance. The Frangipani speaks in a language of scents, whispering tales of love and loss. "The Pontianak," the Frangipani suggests, "is not merely a ghost. She is the pain of loss made manifest. She met her death while giving life.

"From the lore of Southeast Asia, the tale of the Pontianak (or Kuntilanak) takes shape, mainly prevalent in Indonesian, Malay, and Singaporean folklore with variations to her form. She is said to be the soul of a woman who passed away during childbirth and whose spirit remains tethered to the earth by the trauma of her untimely death.

"The name Pontianak likely originates from the Malay language. It is believed to be derived from 'bunting anak' which translates to 'pregnant with child.'

"This spectral entity is a wraith of vengeance and she is as much a part of the landscape as the creeping vines and the mangroves. Her haunting face reflects the land's beauty—a beauty that conceals the obscure in its emerald embrace.

"Beware the beauty that belies the beast, for the Pontianak masquerades as an enchanting maiden with tresses that cascade like nightfall. She is adorned in a kebaya—the traditional dress of Malay women—whose delicate fabric is marred by the somber hue of her death. Her complexion is ghostly, chillingly pallid, and her gaze, ablaze with crimson fury, reveals a voracious longing for vengeance.

"When her facade falters, the true horror is revealed—a countenance contorted by wrath, with sharp fangs and talon-like claws, poised to rend flesh from her unsuspecting prey. She is the predator concealed beneath a deceptive guise.

"In some versions of the folklore, the Pontianak is said to be able to transform into an owl. It is often described as having a distinctive, mournful cry associated with the wails of the Pontianak. The transformation into an owl or another animal is a common motif in many mythologies and folklores, symbolizing the supernatural capabilities of these entities to change shape and move unnoticed among humans.

"Her story is of maternal mortality and she seeks retribution as she tears into the flesh of her victims with her hooklike nails to feast on their organs. Her vengeance is primal, her hunger insatiable as she seeks revenge against men and pregnant women, reflecting deep cultural anxieties about death and the afterlife.

"In the stillness of the night, the paradoxical presence of the Pontianak defies the ordinary laws of sound and distance. She announces her presence through scent and sound. The air thickens with the smell of Frangipani—the sweet fragrance of

Similar Creatures in Folklore

Strigoi
ROMANIA

An undead creature that can transform from human to animal or a hybrid of both. It is the soul of a cursed person who practices black magic and can spread its curse through biting or scratching.

Myling
SCANDINAVIA

The spirits of unbaptized children who seek to compel travelers to bury their bodies properly. They are infamous for their haunting wails and can become dangerous if not appeased.

Langsuir
MALAYSIA

A vampiric ghost of a woman who died while giving birth. Similar to the Pontianak, she can transform into an owl and is known for her long nails and beautiful appearance.

Kuntilanak
INDONESIA

Like the Pontianak, the kuntilanak is a female spirit associated with a woman's death during childbirth. She can also shape-shift into a beautiful woman to lure her prey.

Manananggal
THE PHILIPPINES

A vampiric being capable of severing its own upper body and emerging with wings to soar into the darkness. She preys on pregnant women by sucking the blood of fetuses or newborns.

Churel (page 37)
SOUTH ASIA

The ghost of a woman who died while giving birth or with unfulfilled desires. She is known to return as a vengeful entity, often seeking to drain the vitality of men.

temptation. And then, her cry is a dissonant dirge—a baby's wail, haunting and inconsolable. If it is soft, she is near; if it is loud, she is distant.

"By day, the Pontianak retreats. She resides within banana trees among their broad leaves, shielding her from the sun's gaze. But when night falls, she emerges from her cocoon, her form shifting between beauty and monstrosity. She lures men with promises of desire, only to reveal her true self: a nightmare clad in white.

"It is thought that the Pontianak symbolizes the deep-seated fears surrounding motherhood and the perils of childbirth. This spectral entity is often seen as a cautionary emblem, highlighting the grave risks that women faced historically during pregnancy and labor, times when mortality rates were alarmingly high.

"The narrative of the Pontianak also reflects the societal expectations placed upon women, especially in their traditional roles as mothers and nurturers, representing the collective unresolved grief and trauma associated with maternal deaths.

"It is believed that Pontianak ghost stories have undergone a significant transformation in response to modernization. These narratives originated from traditional beliefs and tales and have been reshaped to resonate with contemporary audiences, reflecting the evolving cultural landscape.

"The image of the Pontianak, once a symbol of fear and superstition, has now found a place in modern mass culture, appearing in various forms of media and entertainment. This evolution signifies folklore's adaptability to contemporary contexts and its enduring relevance in expressing cultural themes.

"Additionally, throughout folklore, the employment of female monstrosity surpasses male fears of female empowerment. It delves into the abject—the unsettling, the grotesque, and the otherworldly. Within this unholy place, the Monstrous Feminine emerges and challenges the stability of symbolic order. The monstrous female embodies the Archaic Mother—a womb that birthed civilizations yet conceals dark secrets. Her maternal embrace is both nurturing and suffocating and within her monstrous womb lies the potential for creation and destruction.

"She also manifests as the vampire—the seductress who wears a beguiling mask of power and draws life force from her victims. Her allure is irresistible and her kiss is both ecstasy and doom. The vampire blurs boundaries: life and death, pleasure and pain.

"Take heed, for I shall share wisdom as enduring as the roots that ground me to the earth. When darkness descends and the birds' song has grown silent, these protection rites against the Pontianak are not just a precaution. They are your only deliverance.

"Shun the solace of solitude, especially under the cloak of night, for the Pontianak lingers there. At your home's threshold lay nails, needles, and scissors. These simple implements are said to stop her in her spectral steps. Drape a cloth of sun-kissed yellow atop your dwelling, a vibrant defense to repel her mournful spirit. Place a bowl of vinegar outside your home, as its pungent aroma is a barrier to her presence.

"Adorn yourself with amulets or charms as each is a defense against her haunting. In the stillness, recite sacred verses, for words of power can dispel the shades she manifests. To defend against the Pontianak, driving a nail into the nape of her neck will render her docile and harmless. Some say she can become a good wife if the nail remains in place! But beware, for her wrath will be released if the nail is ever removed.

"When the Pontianak materializes, you would do best to avoid her fiery gaze. Lower your eyes quickly, lest they penetrate you deeply, for these eyes hold secrets and curses. To meet her stare is to invite evil.

"Remember, wanderer, these are not just superstitions. This advice may be your lifeline in the face of the vengeful spirit. May these time-honored stratagems guide you, sojourner of dusk, and safeguard your passage from the grasp of the Pontianak.

"As you wander the paths of Southeast Asia under the moon's pale light, be mindful of the Pontianak. She manifests the land's sorrow, is a spectator to centuries of stories, and carries the night's innermost secrets."

No Stranger to the Darkness

AUGUST 2023, JOHOR BAHRU, MALAYSIA

During the early morning hours, Johor Bahru is a town transformed, where every alleyway could hide untold stories, and every turn might bring you face-to-face with the unknown.

Officer Qayyum and his coworker patrolled the roads of Johor Bahru's nightfall, where the central vein congealed and slowed the city's heartbeat. The urban expanse stretched before them as dusk's last light and the aborning darkness pulsed with latent energy. Officer Qayyum carried the city's heart within his walkie-talkie. He was no stranger to the darkness; it was his companion.

As the clock chimed 2 a.m., Qayyum and his comrade neared a restricted area in their vehicle. A disturbing sound tore at the silence. It was not a noise that belonged to the world of the living, an ungodly wail that beckoned from the thick undergrowth. Qayyum steered their patrol car toward the source.

The air around Qayyum and his comrade grew dense. As his eyes became accustomed to the lack of light, he scanned the periphery where the jungle met remnants of the old plantation. A rustle, subtle yet distinct—Qayyum's instincts, honed by countless nights under the moon's watchful eye, flared to life.

As he stepped out of the patrol car, leaving his colleague behind, he rested his hand instinctively on the service pistol at his hip. His boots crunched heavily on the gravel as he approached the thicket. A figure emerged, her presence a chilling blend of beauty and horror. She was draped in an ethereal white glow and her hair was a cascade of night. Her eyes were a fiery red that burned with dark malice.

Her movements were unnatural, like a jerky marionette defying the laws of the living. Each motion was a grotesque mimicry of life as if the strings that pulled her were plucked from the sinews of her dead body. Then, with a grotesque grace, she parted her lips and a long, putrid tongue snaked out.

Qayyum understood that he faced a Pontianak, the vampiric spirit of Malay lore.

As she drew closer, the air grew thick with the scent of frangipani. Qayyum's heart thundered in his chest, a frantic drumbeat attempting to rouse him from his spellbound state.

The Pontianak's eyes were now pools of crimson despair, reflecting Qayyum's petrified face. Her fingers were cold and menacing, reaching for him, and her nails grazed his skin with the promise of nightmares made flesh.

With a hand that trembled with fear, Qayyum captured the apparition on his phone and with the suddenness of a night terror, the creature halted her advance. Her eyes, once filled with a ravenous glint, now flared with fear. The hissing that had been the call to her dreadful dance slowed and the night held its breath momentarily. Then she recoiled as if pulled back by some invisible master. Shrouded in darkness, her form retreated with a ghostly elegance. She moved with an ethereal fluidity, her body writhing in impossible ways as she slunk back into the umbra from whence she came.

The hissing faded with her, the sound retreating into a murmur before vanishing altogether.

Just like that, she was gone, leaving only the terrifying memory of her presence and the lingering dread of her return.

The Flying Terror of Malaysia: The Penanggal's Nocturnal Hunt

Another terrifying creature in Malaysian folklore is the penanggal. The penanggal is a type of female vampire that can detach her head from her body and fly around at night, dragging her entrails behind her. She preys on the blood of pregnant women, newborn babies, and corpses. The penanggal is said to be a woman who practices black magic or makes a pact with the devil and uses a special oil or vinegar to separate her head from her body. The penanggal can be detected by the smell of vinegar, the sound of her entrails flapping, or blood around her mouth. She can be killed while her head is away or by using sharp objects, fire, or salt.

Nights of the Kalku

THE CANELO TREE

Nestled in the heart of Chile's diverse terrain, the Canelo tree stands amid the grandeur of the Andes. The landscape here is a vibrant array of ecosystems, from the torrid Atacama Desert in the north to the frozen fjords of the south. The Andes themselves, the creeping spine of the earth that stretches the length of the country, provide a dramatic backdrop to the Canelo's existence.

The Canelo, or Foye, as it is also known, survives and thrives in these contrasting environments. It demonstrates a remarkable adaptability, flourishing where the elements converge. The tree's significance is rooted deeply in Mapuche culture, where it symbolizes the cosmic axis. Its roots are believed to reach the spiritual underworld, while its branches stretch toward the celestial realms.

The Canelo's significance is profound. Under its boughs, it is said that only truth can be spoken, as all weapons and differences must be laid aside. Its leaves grow in cross-shaped clusters and are a living embodiment of peace.

In the Mapuche tradition, the Canelo is a healing tree. Its bark is rich with medicinal properties that have been used for centuries to cure ailments and ward off evil spirits. The tree's presence in ceremonies and rituals underscores its position as a bridge between the earthly and the divine, a connection to the ancestors and the spiritual world. It portrays nature's power and the Mapuche peoples' deep respect for it.

I n the lush valleys of Chile, where the Andes cast their long shadows, the Canelo tree stands as a protector, its branches reaching out to embrace its people. "Listen closely," the Canelo begins, "for my kin and I have stood this ground for centuries. I have seen the Kalku, a figure of Mapuche legend shrouded in the mysteries of the night, so you must heed me well.

"The Kalku, also known as the Calcu, are a prominent feature of Mapuche mythology. They are witches that harness dark magic and manipulate negative energies. They wield their formidable powers in secret, their identities hidden among the populace. No one can truly know who among them is a Kalku, as they blend seamlessly into society by day, only to command the forces of darkness when night falls.

"Kalku move with the silence of the falling dusk. Their eyes are like the darkest pits of the earth, voids that consume all light. Their hands are contorted like the roots of ancient trees as they cast spells that twist reality. They work with wekufe, wicked creatures, or spirits such as the anchimayen—tiny spirit helpers—or the chonchon—a bird-like entity with a human head and feathers made of human hair, said to be the Kalku's magical incarnation. The chonchon is comparable to a witch's familiar in European witchcraft traditions, serving its Kalku master as a supernatural assistant. These servants are summoned to inflict harm, spread disease, and sow discord in society, moving through the night to carry out their master's malevolent will.

"Kalku are the unseen architects of chaos, orchestrating calamities and curses that befall unsuspecting communities. So terrifying is their reputation that even speaking their name is believed to invite misfortune.

"In contrast, the Machi is a traditional healer and spiritual leader. The Machi are considered benevolent, playing significant roles in the Mapuche religion. The purpose of the Machi is to help their community through healing rituals like machitún or mapundugún, where they communicate with the spiritual world to reveal causes of illness or misfortune and remedy them.

"Both Kalku and Machi share traits similar to what anthropologists would consider a shaman—a spiritual leader with supernatural privileges and knowledge of natural medicine. However, their intentions and methods differ significantly, reflecting the dualistic nature of Mapuche spirituality.

"Typically, a Kalku inherits their position, but they can also be an irritated Machi who disobeys Mapuche laws. They often deviate from these precepts and use their abilities for their own gain or to harm others.

"The Kalku's actions are believed to cause illnesses and unfortunate events, making them figures of fear and respect within Mapuche culture. Local communities rely on

Similar Creatures in Folklore

Yee Naaldlooshii (Skinwalker) (pages 45 and 141)
NAVAJO

A type of harmful witch known as a skinwalker who can transform into animals and is feared for their malevolent acts.

Darana
AUSTRALIAN ABORIGINAL

A mythological figure often associated with dark magic and sorcery.

Bruja/Brujo
HISPANOSPHERE

Witches who may use their powers for good or ill, paralleling the dual nature of the Kalku's magic.

Manitou
ALGONQUIAN

Spirits that encompass both benevolent and malevolent aspects, reflecting the Kalku's complex nature.

Bokor (male) or Caplata (female)
HAITIAN VODOU

Sorcerers who are known for practicing both helpful and harmful magic, much like the Kalku.

Abathakathi (page 77)
ZULU

They share the Kalku's potential for powerful dark sorcery.

ritual healers and diviners such as the Machi to counteract malevolent spells cast by these dark sorcerers.

"The Mapuches' profound connection to the mapu, or land, is the cornerstone of their existence and the muse for their myths. This bond is reflected in their reverence for nature, the cycles of life, and the universal forces that govern them. The Kalku, as a figure of power and mystery, embodies the darker aspects of these forces, serving as a counterbalance to the benevolent spirits and deities in the Mapuche pantheon. The Kalku's existence reminds the Mapuche of the delicate equilibrium between good and evil, order and chaos, and the ever-present dance between light and shadow. As the Canelo, I have connected the Mapuche people to the spiritual world. Around me, they perform their sacred ceremonies, seeking the guidance of their spiritual leaders, who, unlike the Kalku, use their knowledge and power for healing and maintaining the cosmic balance.

"The folklore of the Kalku emerged from Mapuche mythology as a representation of sorcery and dark spiritual forces. Academically, it's understood that these figures were often used by local authorities and ritual specialists to express their views on sorcery and to develop strategies to counteract those they accused of being Kalku. Essentially, the Kalku became a symbol for explaining mysterious or unfortunate events, and accusations could serve to control or influence social and political situations within the community. This role in folklore reflects broader themes of power, influence, and the human need to understand and manage the unknown.

"Historically, the Mapuche have faced adversities and conflicts, which undoubtedly influenced their folklore. The struggles against colonization and the subsequent need to protect their territory and way of life may have given rise to the Kalku— now a protector of sorts, albeit through darker means. Kalku's role as a disruptor could also be seen as a metaphor for Mapuche resistance to external threats.

"Moreover, the Mapuches' intricate social and spiritual systems, including the roles of the Machi and the community's healers, have likely shaped the Kalku's narrative. The Machi, who mediates between the physical and spiritual realms, contrasts with the Kalku to create a dynamic interplay.

"In essence, the folklore of the Kalku mirrors the Mapuches' innermost values and fears. The story has evolved with the people, reflecting their history, struggles, and fighting spirit. It is a tale not just of magic and might but of identity and endurance.

"To protect oneself from the Kalku's malevolent grasp, one must turn to the wisdom of the Canelo. My leaves can cleanse the soul and my wood can repel the darkest curses. Craft a talisman from my bark, carry a leaf in your pocket, or simply rest beneath my canopy. In doing so, you align yourself with the forces of life and purity, creating a barrier through which the Kalku cannot pass.

"Remember, the Kalku preys on the isolated and the weak. Stand together, for unity is strength, and strength is protection. Let the laughter of children and the songs of elders fill the air, for these sounds are anathema to the Kalku.

"As long as the Canelo stands, the Kalku will linger only in the shadows, never daring to enter the light.

"As the sun dips below the horizon, it casts a golden glow upon the land and the Mapuche gather beneath my outstretched limbs. They stand united, their eyes reflecting the last light of day, their spirits linked intrinsically with the natural world. In this moment, the Kalku's power wanes, for it cannot thrive where there is light, love, and the strength of a people rooted in their traditions."

We Are the Keepers of Balance

APRIL 2019, SALAMANCA, CHILE

North of Salamanca looms the Raja de Manquehua, a legendary mountain over 6,500 feet (2,000 m) high. The mountain's south face bears an extensive crack—called La Raja—which leads into a mysterious chasm. This is no ordinary cave; it is the Cueva de los Brujos—the Cave of the Sorcerers. This rocky crevice, resembling a deep ravine, is notoriously difficult to access. For decades, it has allegedly served as a gathering place for witches who convene there to practice dark magic.

Young Luca followed a path winding through tangled underbrush as he approached La Raja. The entrance gaped wide, its darkness hungry. He clutched his phone, its feeble light swallowed by the yawning cavern.

Luca had heard tales of the cave, and curiosity had gnawed at his insides like a famished rat. For Luca's school days were a torment—a relentless barrage of taunts and jeers. He sought refuge in the library, where the books held power, full of forgotten spells and ancient sorcery. Luca devoured them, his fingers tracing faded ink. He learned of the Kalku, who worked with shadows.

Luca hungered for more knowledge. He yearned for the Kalku's power. The bullies would pay. Their laughter would turn to screams.

Now, the crevice beckoned him. Luca hesitated. The bullies' laughter replayed in his mind—their taunts, their jeers.

And so, Luca crawled into the Raja de Manquehua, like a worm inching toward enlightenment.

Luca's light traced the hidden chambers. Was it his imagination, or did the shadows shift? A glint of eyes met his. Luca froze, his heart pounding.

And then creatures emerged from the cavernous depths—Kalku, their twisted forms half-rooted in stone.

Their limbs contorted, reaching for him. Their breath rasped as a chorus of hunger and yearning. He inched backward, but the cave tightened its grip.

Luca had no choice but to watch as the creatures danced, their movements both grotesque and mesmerizing.

The Kalku's misshapen bodies shifted, their eyes never leaving Luca's.

"Luca, seeker of dark magic," they said, "we see your pain. The bullies at school—their taunts, their cruelty. We are the keepers of balance."

Luca's breaths came in ragged gasps as the starved ancients pulled at his being. Their fingers pressed against his skin. And then the whispers began—an onslaught of overlapping and indistinct voices.

The cavern's air thickened as the Kalku descended upon him. One of them leaned in close. Its icy and foul breath seeped into Luca's lungs.

He felt it then—the insidious pull. His life force, once vibrant, was now sucked from his body. The Kalku's lips grazed his, and with each inhale, she drained him.

The Kalku's hunger knew no bounds. As they chanted incantations, the life force transformed into luminous spheres. These ethereal lights pirouetted upward. The Kalku devoured the dancing lights.

But Luca did not die on this night. Within the cave lay the souls of deceased sorcerers, their spirits imbuing initiates with newfound powers.

Luca, drawn by fate, stepped into the cavern, where his original soul was replaced by a new one infused with ancient magic.

Guardians in the Grain: The Hidden History of Witch Marks

Witch marks, or apotropaic marks, are symbols inscribed onto woodwork or stone close to a building's entrances. These marks are found predominantly in the United Kingdom, but they can be discovered in other areas of Europe. Contrary to their name, witch markings are not explicitly associated with witches or witchcraft. Instead, they served as powerful protective symbols, turning away evil and ensuring safety for those within the building. This unique function of witch marks offers a fascinating insight into the supernatural beliefs and protective symbols of the past.

The Watery Realm of the Njuzu

THE MUHACHA TREE

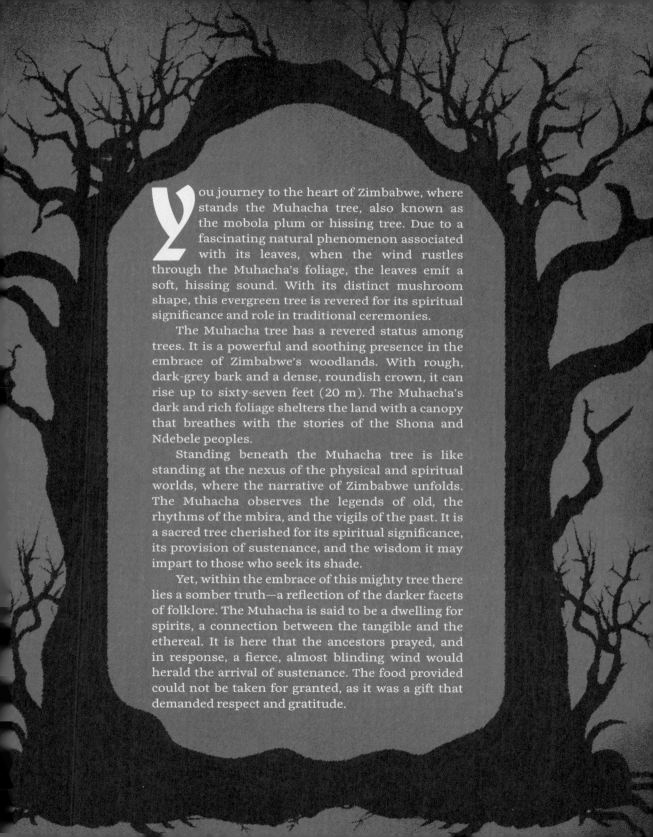

Y ou journey to the heart of Zimbabwe, where stands the Muhacha tree, also known as the mobola plum or hissing tree. Due to a fascinating natural phenomenon associated with its leaves, when the wind rustles through the Muhacha's foliage, the leaves emit a soft, hissing sound. With its distinct mushroom shape, this evergreen tree is revered for its spiritual significance and role in traditional ceremonies.

The Muhacha tree has a revered status among trees. It is a powerful and soothing presence in the embrace of Zimbabwe's woodlands. With rough, dark-grey bark and a dense, roundish crown, it can rise up to sixty-seven feet (20 m). The Muhacha's dark and rich foliage shelters the land with a canopy that breathes with the stories of the Shona and Ndebele peoples.

Standing beneath the Muhacha tree is like standing at the nexus of the physical and spiritual worlds, where the narrative of Zimbabwe unfolds. The Muhacha observes the legends of old, the rhythms of the mbira, and the vigils of the past. It is a sacred tree cherished for its spiritual significance, its provision of sustenance, and the wisdom it may impart to those who seek its shade.

Yet, within the embrace of this mighty tree there lies a somber truth—a reflection of the darker facets of folklore. The Muhacha is said to be a dwelling for spirits, a connection between the tangible and the ethereal. It is here that the ancestors prayed, and in response, a fierce, almost blinding wind would herald the arrival of sustenance. The food provided could not be taken for granted, as it was a gift that demanded respect and gratitude.

Y ou rest upon the gnarled roots of the ancient Muhacha. Its whispers rise with the evening mist. "The Njuzu," the ancient tree hisses, "are not mere dwellers of the deep. They are the sovereigns of storm and stillness, the architects of the heavens' tears, the guardians of depths now scorned, and the mourners of sacred pacts broken by human neglect. The sculptors of the river's rage, they reflect water's forsaken grace.

"In the lore of the Shona and Ndebele peoples of Zimbabwe and some communities in Mozambique and South Africa, the Njuzu reign—a mesmerizing force of water spirits. Their dominion extends beyond the liquid embrace of Southern Africa's waters and they are often held responsible for unexplained events—inclement weather, natural disasters, and the disappearance of people.

"While not described in detail, the Njuzu are often imagined as beautiful and enchanting. These aquatic beings transcend gender—they are both mermaids and mermen. Their skin shimmers like the surface of a sunlit pond and their hair flows like the river currents. But do not be fooled by their enchanting appearance, for their eyes hold the depth of the oceans. The Njuzu can be diabolical creatures; their presence is felt in the rustling reeds and the ripples of moonlight.

"They summon the rain with a flick of their iridescent tails and bless the parched soil with life's elixir. Their laughter ripples across the sky, birthing rainbows that arch in a beautiful array of colors. Yet, when scorned by humans' actions, their wrath unfurls in torrents, their sorrow cascading as relentless downpours that swell rivers and reshape landscapes.

"The Njuzu are guardians of the aquatic threshold and are known to drag people into their watery kingdoms. Their song is a siren's call, a melody with the allure of the unknown and the promise of forbidden knowledge. Those who succumb to their enchantment find themselves ensnared, not by chains, but by the cold embrace of the water's depths.

"With their dual nature, these spirits are both the givers and takers of breath. They pull the defiant beneath the surface, where the world is a blur of green and blue and silence reigns. Here, in the Njuzu's domain, the secrets of the waters are revealed, tales of ancient pacts and the sacred bond between spirit and mortal.

"Yet, the Njuzu's grasp is not always one of malice. To those who approach with respect, they offer glimpses of the water's wisdom, the understanding of currents that carve the earth, and the tides that govern the moon. They teach the language of the seas and the ebbs and flows of life.

"Respect the Njuzu, for they are the soul of the waters. Honor their domain and the rains will come. Neglect their wisdom and the floods will rise. They are not mere

Similar Creatures in Folklore

Mermaid/Merman
GLOBAL

Half-human, half-fish beings that live in the ocean and can be benevolent or malevolent to humans.

Selkie (page 45)
SCOTLAND AND IRELAND

Selkies are mythical creatures that transform from seals to humans by shedding their skin. Their ability to return to seal form depends on reclaiming this skin.

Rusalka
SLAVIC FOLKLORE

Water nymphs or spirits associated with lakes or rivers, often linked to the fate of drowned women.

Siren
ANCIENT GREECE

Creatures with the upper half and face of a woman and the lower body of a bird. They are also known for their enchanting singing that lures sailors to their doom.

Kelpie
SCOTLAND

Shape-shifting water spirits that can appear as horses or humans, known to lure people into the water.

Jengu
SAWA, CAMEROON

Mermaid-like water spirits thought to bestow healing and good fortune upon their devotees.

Yara
BRAZIL

Also known as Iara, this is a water nymph with green hair and fair skin who is known to enchant men and lure them to live underwater.

folklore; they are the pulse of the waters, the rhythm of the rain, and the keepers of the storm.

"In the fading tales of Zimbabwean lore, where streams once sang and pools held the reflection of the stars, the Njuzu's call is heard. In the heart of Southern Africa, where the waters once ran pure, their voices now murmur with a mix of melancholy and wrath. They are also the spirits of those who perished in the depths, their essence now entwined with watery wastelands of neglect. Once revered for their power to summon rain and bestow blessings, these beings now watch as their sanctuaries are defiled by the corruption of money.

"Your scholars define the Njuzu and other water spirits as central figures in folklore, particularly in Zimbabwean mythology. These spirits are often seen as guardians of the natural environment, with roles that include rainmaking and promoting conservation efforts within communities. The Njuzu, in particular, are sometimes associated with mysterious occurrences around water bodies, such as blocking water pipes or appearing at dam sites, which sparks debates on their influence on natural conservation efforts.

"The Njuzu are worshipped as ancestral spirits because they are believed to possess individuals, initiating them into roles such as herbalists or traditional healers, which are highly respected within the community. This connection to important community roles likely contributes to their reverence as ancestors. Additionally, water is a source of life and sustenance, so spirits associated with water may naturally be held in high esteem and considered protectors or benefactors of the people. They embody the water—ancient, ever-flowing, and unpredictable. As guardians, they watch over their descendants and the land they cherish. Their wisdom flows like the rivers, guiding humanity through life's currents. The Njuzu embody continuity. Their whispers are heard in the babbling brooks and the thunderous waterfalls. When storms brew and rivers swell, blame the Njuzu. They control the elements, and their moods are reflected in the changing skies.

"Njuzu folklore is an integral part of Zimbabwean culture, connecting humanity to the natural world. It reminds the community that they are mere stewards of the land and have been entrusted with its care. In stories told around campfires, the Njuzu dance between reverence and fear. Their existence serves as a cautionary tale—a reminder that water, like life, demands respect.

"To protect oneself from the fickle whims of the Njuzu, offerings once made to honor them now serve as a plea for forgiveness. Respect for the water and adherence to traditional rituals were once paramount but now serve as a desperate attempt to mend the bond, as the Njuzu's once formidable power has faded with the light.

"So, my friend, as you traverse the landscapes of Zimbabwe under the vast African sky, remember the Njuzu. They are the whisper of the waves, the reflection in the water, the keepers of ancient wisdom now forgotten. Your respect for their domain, once a source of blessings, is now a plea to stop your meddling. The Njuzu are the soul of the waters, the guardians of life's ebb and flow, now yearning for the weavers of fate to return."

Honor Us

MAY 2017, ZIMBABWE, AFRICA

In the lands of Zimbabwe, the Osborne Dam looms, and there, amid the machinery and the ceaseless hum of generators, toiled a young engineer named Tendai. He was a man of science—a believer in equations, Newton's laws, and the tangible world. Folklore, he scoffed, was for the superstitious and the uneducated.

Yet, strange occurrences plagued Tendai's work as the days turned into weeks. The pumps malfunctioned without rhyme or reason. Wrenches vanished, only to reappear in bizarre locations. And whispers—soft as the breeze—swept across the dam.

His colleague, Chikwava, raised an eyebrow. "Njuzu," he muttered, his voice thick with reverence. "Water spirits. They guard this place."

Tendai scoffed. "Superstitions," he retorted.

But one moonless night, as Tendai adjusted a faulty valve, he heard a haunting melody. The water seemed to vibrate, its surface shimmering with a luminescent glow. Tendai's heart quickened and he knew he was no longer alone.

There they were: two Njuzu, their forms half-submerged in the dam's depths. Their eyes fixed upon him. Their skin was translucent as moonlight, revealing sinuous tails that flicked like eels. Tendai's breath caught as he moved closer to the water's edge.

The Njuzu flitted through the water.

"Listen," they sang, their voices like wind chimes. "We are the daughters of the river, the keepers of stories. We remember when the world was young and the old gods walked the earth."

Tendai leaned closer, entranced. He smiled, forgetting the pumps and the malfunctioning valves. The Njuzu's eyes held no malice; they were almost tender.

"Step," they urged, but their mouths opened wider—gaping maws that defied anatomy. Rows of teeth that were serrated and iridescent lined their throats.

Their voices wove through Tendai's mind. Desperate to drown out the noises, he clenched his head and tangled his fingers in his hair.

"Come," their breathy voices twining like serpents. "Come, mortal child of earth and air."

He swayed, teetering on the precipice. The Njuzu's eyes flared and light streamed forth. Their song intensified, a maddening crescendo. Tendai's skin prickled and he tasted salt on his lips as if the dam itself wept.

"Come," they urged, their mouths opening wider. "Come into our embrace. Honor us."

And he almost did—the dam beckoned, lapping at the edge. The Njuzu leaned closer, their teeth elongated and gnashed like millstones.

But then, Chikwava materialized, and his voice cut through the madness. "Tendai!" he shouted, shaking Tendai's body.

Tendai blinked, the Njuzu's spell broken. Chikwava's eyes held concern as he pulled Tendai away from the water. The spirits vanished, leaving only ripples on the surface.

"What did you see?" Chikwava asked, oblivious to the horror that had unfolded.

Tendai's gaze lingered on the water. "The truth," he whispered.

The Siren's Call: The Tale of Zennor's Enchanted Mermaid

One of the most popular stories of a mermaid in Cornish folklore is that of the Mermaid of Zennor. According to the legend, a beautiful and mysterious woman would occasionally attend the church of St. Senara in the village of Zennor, Cornwall, England and enchant the parishioners with her lovely voice. Mathey Trewella, a young man who was the village's greatest singer, piqued her curiosity. One day, he followed her to the sea and never returned. Years later, a mermaid appeared on a ship near the coast and asked them to raise their anchor, as it was blocking the entrance to her home, where she lived with her husband Mathey and their children. The villagers realized that the mermaid was the same woman who had visited their church, and they carved a mermaid figure on a wooden bench to commemorate the story.

The Fleshgait's Deception

THE QUAKING ASPEN TREE

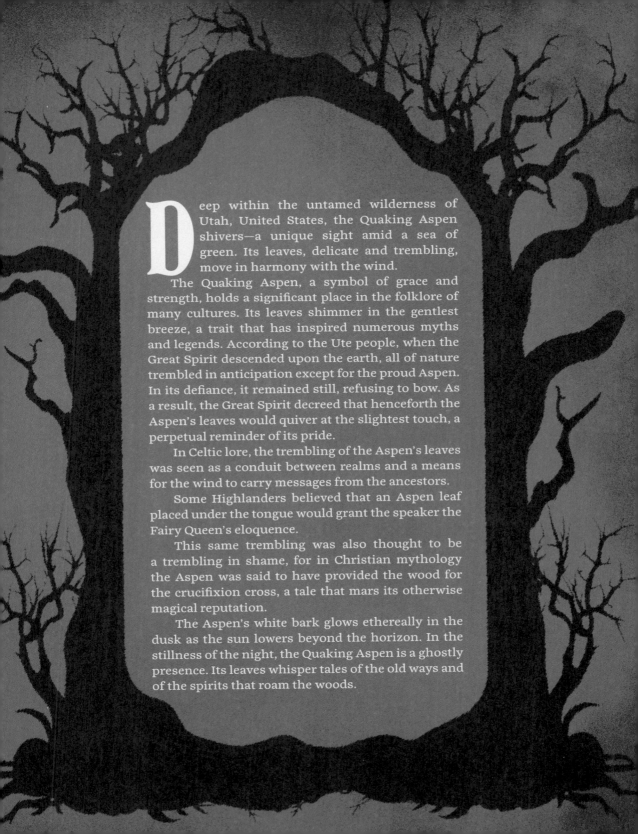

Deep within the untamed wilderness of Utah, United States, the Quaking Aspen shivers—a unique sight amid a sea of green. Its leaves, delicate and trembling, move in harmony with the wind.

The Quaking Aspen, a symbol of grace and strength, holds a significant place in the folklore of many cultures. Its leaves shimmer in the gentlest breeze, a trait that has inspired numerous myths and legends. According to the Ute people, when the Great Spirit descended upon the earth, all of nature trembled in anticipation except for the proud Aspen. In its defiance, it remained still, refusing to bow. As a result, the Great Spirit decreed that henceforth the Aspen's leaves would quiver at the slightest touch, a perpetual reminder of its pride.

In Celtic lore, the trembling of the Aspen's leaves was seen as a conduit between realms and a means for the wind to carry messages from the ancestors.

Some Highlanders believed that an Aspen leaf placed under the tongue would grant the speaker the Fairy Queen's eloquence.

This same trembling was also thought to be a trembling in shame, for in Christian mythology the Aspen was said to have provided the wood for the crucifixion cross, a tale that mars its otherwise magical reputation.

The Aspen's white bark glows ethereally in the dusk as the sun lowers beyond the horizon. In the stillness of the night, the Quaking Aspen is a ghostly presence. Its leaves whisper tales of the old ways and of the spirits that roam the woods.

Y ou rest your back against the slender trunk of the Quaking Aspen, its leaves a mosaic of warm autumn hues, contrasting its white branches that stretch like bony fingers. The tree's shadow is elongated and sinuous, whispering its narrative in a stirring, evocative voice. As you close your eyes, the leaves begin their tremulous dance, and the Aspen confides. "The Fleshgait," the tree reveals, "is not just a mimic. It reflects your fears, the duality of what is known and unknown, and the reminder of the thin line between self and other.

"From the realms of online folklore the Fleshgait emerges, embodying what many believe a skinwalker to be: a chimeric entity that bears the traits of myriad creatures. This shape-shifter adopts the guise of those it encounters.

"To face the Fleshgait is to confront your worst fears. It is the darkness that speaks with stolen voices and nightmare made flesh. It is the uncanny made manifest, the terror that wears a trusted visage, and the darkness that beckons with a loved one's voice. Beware, for the Fleshgait is not a creature of the night. It is the dark night itself.

"When the Fleshgait dons the guise of humanity, it becomes a marionette of flesh, and its movements are a grotesque pantomime of life. With jerky gesticulations, the Fleshgait beckons its prey to follow it into the seclusion of the woods, perhaps to consume or clothe itself in its victim's skin at a time of its choosing. Its charade is fleeting, for it has not yet learned the art of being among humans.

"For the Fleshgait, mimicry is a superficial craft. It can parrot the human form and replicate the sounds of speech, but the subtleties of being—the flicker of emotion and the dance of interaction—are beyond its grasp. To emulate is not to understand; thus, the Fleshgait remains an outsider, a watcher on the periphery of human existence, forever looking in but never truly seeing.

"Emerging from the forest's shadow, the victim bears a hollow resemblance to their former self. Stripped of the vibrancy that once defined them, they are rendered mute in the language of emotion, their expressions vacant, their opinions silenced. Once a river of thought, their speech is now a stagnant pool. They can only mimic the words and sounds they have heard.

"In the darkness of the forest, the Fleshgait undergoes its metamorphosis. It is a mesmerizing and macabre spectacle as the creature sheds its borrowed form, not unlike a serpent discarding its skin. The detritus of a thousand stolen bodies lay scattered across the ground. The Fleshgait contorts. With each ripple of its flesh, it casts off humanity's face, revealing its proper form's raw essence. It is a dance of shadows and substance, a ritual of rebirth that speaks of the ancient and the arcane.

Similar Creatures in Folklore

Doppelgänger
GERMANY

A malevolent double that looks and sounds exactly like the person they are mimicking. Seeing one's doppelgänger is said to be an omen of death or disaster.

Yee Naaldlooshii (Skinwalker) (pages 45 and 125)
NAVAJO

A witch who has the ability to turn into any chosen animal by wearing its hide. Skinwalkers can also mimic the voice of their prey or anyone they have killed.

Tsukumogami
JAPAN

Objects that come to life after one hundred years, tsukumogami can take on human form, speak, and sometimes cause mischief or harm to humans.

Púca/Pooka (page 45)
IRELAND

Creatures that can take on the form of a horse, goat, rabbit, or human. Púcas can also speak in human language and sometimes help or trick humans.

"As the Fleshgait's new form takes shape, it reminds you of myth's mutable nature. It is ongoing evidence of the stories you tell and the creatures you conjure from the depths of your collective imagination. In the end, the Fleshgait is not just a creature of change, it is change itself—the embodiment of the ever-evolving narrative of the night.

"As online stories began to diverge from authentic skinwalker legends, a new term was needed to describe these entities accurately. Thus, 'Fleshgait' was coined, combining synonyms for 'skin' and 'walk' to create a distinct label for these creatures of modern myth. The term encapsulates the idea of a being that can mimic human appearance and voice by watching or stealing a person's skin, but that cannot recreate perfectly their behavior or memories.

"This linguistic evolution reflects the broader trend of folklore adapting to the digital age. Stories and myths are shared and reshaped across the internet, creating new terms and legends like the Fleshgait.

"Some online fables claim they are tormented spirits or malevolent entities from the woods, while others speculate they may be cryptids, creatures of flesh and blood that have defied discovery.

"The lore of the Fleshgait blends ancient myths, psychological fears, and the transformative power of storytelling. In the digital age, folklore has transcended its traditional boundaries, evolving into a form that is shared and reshaped across the internet. As your scholars have noted, digital folklore converges with computer-mediated communication, giving rise to new forms of vernacular creativity and memetics. The old stories find new life in the binary realms of cyberspace, where they are preserved and transformed.

"The Fleshgait is a digital specter, its legend spread via online forums and social media. It is evidence of folklore's adaptability, reflecting your collective fears and curiosities in a medium that transcends geographic and cultural barriers.

"As you engage with these modern myths, you participate in a global conversation that shapes and redefines them. The Fleshgait is no longer solely a figure of the local lore of North America; it has become a part of a larger narrative, written continuously by countless anonymous authors on the vast canvas of the internet.

"This new chapter in the story of folklore is marked by a profound shift—a democratization of narrative creation. No longer are tales passed down solely through generations; they are now created, disseminated, and modified by anyone with access to the digital world. The Fleshgait's evolution from whispered legend to an online phenomenon is emblematic of this shift—a shift that has seen folklore become a living, breathing entity in the age of algorithms. This shift should give you hope for the future of folklore, as it ensures its continuous growth and adaptation.

"To protect yourself from the Fleshgait, you must be vigilant. Trust your instincts—if a voice or figure in the woods seems off, this creature could entice you into its trap. It is said that it cannot imitate a voice it has not heard, so be wary of any familiar call that comes without context. Stay in groups, as the Fleshgait is less likely to attack when multiple potential victims exist. And always carry a source of light, as the creature is known to be repelled by brightness.

"Traveler of the whispering woods, be cautious as you venture into the wilderness. The Fleshgait embodies the uncanny, the terror that wears a trusted face, the darkness that speaks with stolen voices. It is a reminder of the dangers that lurk in the shadows.

"Let these cautions be your compass, sojourner of the shaded paths, and may your journey through the woods remain untouched by the guile of the Fleshgait."

The Night Minion

AUGUST 2018, PLEASANT GROVE, UTAH, UNITED STATES

In the stillness of the night, Bob Sheldon's journey home was about to descend into madness. The clock had just struck 12:05 a.m. and the world lay quiet, save for the hum of his car's engine.

Just as he was about to make the customary left turn onto 700 South, the headlights illuminated a creature scuttling across the street on all fours. Bob eased off the accelerator instinctively, his mind struggling to process the form of . . . a stray cat?

Bob's knuckles paled as he gripped the steering wheel, the beams of his headlights slicing through the ominous dark night to reveal something far more sinister than a cat. The sight before him was a perversion of nature, a creature that scurried across the pavement with a horrifying fluidity that opposed its grotesque form. Its limbs, too long and angular for any earthly being, moved with disturbing synchronicity, propelling it forward in such a way that seemed to mock the very concept of gravity.

The sound of its movement was a nightmarish cacophony, claws scraping against the ground in a rhythm that mimicked Bob's erratic heartbeat. This sound would haunt the edges of his dreams and be at the forefront of his nightmares, a reminder of the night when reality twisted into a grotesque parody.

As the creature reached the safety of the other side, it rose. The action was smooth, almost rehearsed as if it had performed this macabre performance countless times before. Its body unfolded, unfurled, tall and thin, towering over Bob's car.

It was one of the night's minions. Its eyes, reflecting the headlights, burned with a profane light, fixing Bob with a stare that promised eons of the abyss. It took Bob a moment to realize that he was looking at a distorted and contorted version of himself.

The sight was petrifying, a grotesque reflection that twisted his features into an expression of eternal torment. And then, to Bob's horror, the creature smiled, its teeth jagged—a chilling, knowing smile that seemed to say it had been waiting for him a very long time.

A primitive fear seized Bob as the creature's gaze held him captive. It was a look that knew him, that saw through the facade of his humanity to the vulnerable flesh beneath. At that moment, Bob was nothing more than prey. He was meat in the sight of a predator.

The air grew cold, a chill that seeped into his bones. The world around him dimmed, the creature's presence a black hole that absorbed all warmth, all optimism. Bob's mind screamed for him to flee, to escape the horror that stood watching on 700 South.

But he was frozen, trapped in the headlights' glow with a creature that defied explanation. A being that should not exist—yet there it was, a terror made flesh and bone on a quiet street in Pleasant Grove.

The sudden noise of a passing car from the other direction snapped Bob to his senses. He put his foot on the gas pedal and the streets became a blur as Bob raced toward the sanctuary of home, his mind replaying the tales he had dismissed as mere ghost stories. The creature's image was seared into his memory, a harbinger of the unknown that stalked the edges of Pleasant Grove.

The Serpent of the Frontier: The Myth of the Bear Lake Monster

The creature known as the Bear Lake Monster comes from the folklore of the Utah-Idaho border area around Bear Lake. In the nineteenth century, Joseph C. Rich, a Mormon settler, wrote articles about second-hand sightings of a serpent-like creature in the lake. These stories were published in the *Deseret News* in 1868, sparking interest and debate among the local populace.

Descriptions of the Bear Lake Monster are varied, though it is often portrayed as a colossal serpent, endowed with legs that allow it to traverse both land and water with astonishing speed. Some accounts liken its head to that of a cow, otter, crocodile, or walrus, and its length is estimated to be a staggering forty to fifty feet (12 to 15 m). Reports even speak of menacing spikes adorning its back.

Interest in this creature has fluctuated over the years, with the last reported sighting occurring in 2002.

Ötzi's Curse

THE EUROPEAN LARCH TREE

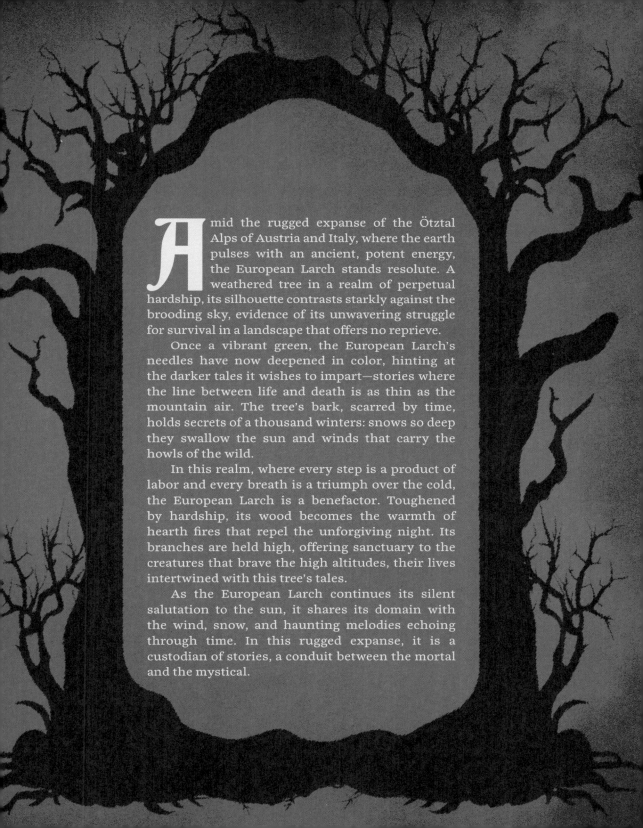

Amid the rugged expanse of the Ötztal Alps of Austria and Italy, where the earth pulses with an ancient, potent energy, the European Larch stands resolute. A weathered tree in a realm of perpetual hardship, its silhouette contrasts starkly against the brooding sky, evidence of its unwavering struggle for survival in a landscape that offers no reprieve.

Once a vibrant green, the European Larch's needles have now deepened in color, hinting at the darker tales it wishes to impart—stories where the line between life and death is as thin as the mountain air. The tree's bark, scarred by time, holds secrets of a thousand winters: snows so deep they swallow the sun and winds that carry the howls of the wild.

In this realm, where every step is a product of labor and every breath is a triumph over the cold, the European Larch is a benefactor. Toughened by hardship, its wood becomes the warmth of hearth fires that repel the unforgiving night. Its branches are held high, offering sanctuary to the creatures that brave the high altitudes, their lives intertwined with this tree's tales.

As the European Larch continues its silent salutation to the sun, it shares its domain with the wind, snow, and haunting melodies echoing through time. In this rugged expanse, it is a custodian of stories, a conduit between the mortal and the mystical.

s you gaze at the gathering snowflakes, you notice an Alpine chamois. Nimble and unassuming, it freezes suddenly, sensing the charged air. Its eyes lock with yours, a visceral warning before it bounds away. Your gaze returns to the European Larch, where a single snowflake lands on one of its needles, its unique structure glistening in the cool, faint light. Stoic and enduring, the tree shares its knowledge in a voice that crackles like thin ice. "The Ötzi curse," it whispers, a chill in its timbre, "is not merely a legend. It embodies ancient transgressions, the silent screams of history's forgotten, and the weight of retribution for those who dare disturb the slumber of the past.

"In the dark recesses of human belief, where the supernatural breathes and the unknown seethes, curses take form—a potent force in folklore and myth. Curses are as ancient as fear of the dark, manifesting the power of words and will. They are invoked to bring misfortune, illness, and death, often as retribution for wrongdoing or to exact revenge. Your kind believes in curses because they embody the human tendency to find meaningful patterns in random events, to ascribe a cause to chaos, and to seek answers for those things that cannot be explained. This psychological phenomenon—where a belief in curses is often reinforced by the tendency to associate general misfortune with personally significant jinxes—is known as the Barnum or Forer Effect. In this way, you become architects of your own doom.

"In the shadowy realm of superstition and the supernatural, where fear and mystery intertwine, the curse of Ötzi stands as a chilling example of the power of ancient hexes and confirmation bias—a force rooted deeply in folklore and history.

"On September 19, 1991, a remarkable discovery was made by German hikers whilst walking the Ötztal Alps. When they reached the boundary between Italy and Austria, they stumbled across what they initially thought was the corpse of a modern-day human. However, it soon became apparent they had happened upon a sensational archaeological find—the well-preserved body of a man who had lived during the Copper Age (an archaeological period marked by the increased use of smelted copper). The remains would later become known as Ötzi, or the Iceman, and he had lived between the years 3350 and 3105 BCE.

"The Iceman died violently: He had been shot in the back with an arrow, which struck a main artery. This injury would have caused him to bleed to death within minutes. The cold conditions at the high altitude where he lay down to die led to his body being preserved in the ice for millennia, providing an unprecedented window into the past.

"Following the discovery of Ötzi, a pattern of misfortune began to emerge. Several people linked to Ötzi—the hikers who found him, a mountaineer who filmed him, scientists who examined him, and others—died under circumstances that some

Other Curses in Folklore

Annabelle
CONNECTICUT, UNITED STATES

Annabelle is a Raggedy Ann doll said to be possessed by the spirit of a young girl. It became one of the most famous cases investigated by Ed and Lorraine Warren, renowned paranormal investigators and authors. The doll was housed in the now-closed Warren's Occult Museum in Connecticut, United States.

Robert the Doll
FLORIDA, UNITED STATES

A doll that allegedly moves on its own and brings misfortune, displayed at the Fort East Martello Museum.

The Phone Number 0888-888-888
BULGARIA

A Bulgarian phone number associated with the untimely demise of its owners, now out of service.

Thomas Busby's Chair
ENGLAND

The "Dead Man's Chair," said to bring death to anyone who sits in it, is hung from the ceiling at the Thirsk Museum in Thirsk, North Yorkshire, to prevent use.

The Anguished Man
ENGLAND

A painting that is said to contain the spirit of the artist's relative, who mixed his own blood into the paint, causing strange occurrences.

The Dybbuk Box
EASTERN EUROPE

A wine cabinet haunted by a dybbuk, an evil spirit from Jewish folklore known for causing nightmares and health issues.

The Hope Diamond
INDIA

A gemstone carrying the legend of a curse that brings misfortune to its owners; it is now housed at the Smithsonian Natural History Museum in Washington, DC, United States.

considered mysterious or untimely. This series of deaths fueled speculation about a curse associated with the Iceman's remains.

"The notion of a curse gained traction as each new death added to the legend, creating a narrative that seemed to encompass ancient warnings about disturbing the rest of the deceased. Whether these events are mere coincidences or something more sinister is a matter of personal belief, but they have undoubtedly contributed to the mystery surrounding Ötzi and his legacy.

"Curses like that of Ötzi lack physical substance, dwelling instead in the ethereal realms of incantations and omens. They are the silent scourge, the foreboding omen, and the dreaded repercussion for those who dare disturb sacred relics or ancient remains. The nocebo effect mirrors this concept, where negative expectations can lead to real suffering without any physical cause—just as belief sustains a curse's potency, so does the anticipation of harm bring about genuine affliction.

"Throughout history, curses have been woven through narratives of envy, wrath, avarice, and vengeance. They serve as warnings against harboring dark sentiments and deeds. In every culture's lore, curses emerge as a universal motif—a reflection of the powerful interplay between dread and belief that shapes your stories.

"As a guardian against such ancient curses, you must understand that they often hinge on specific conditions. Their dissolution lies in meeting these terms. Whether it involves returning stolen artifacts or appeasing disturbed spirits, liberation's key is frequently concealed within plain view.

"The curse of Ötzi is said to be linked to his mortal remains—a body preserved by ice and time. To sever this connection could mean dispelling the curse, unraveling the enchantment laid long ago, and potentially reversing its grim effects.

"Craft yourself amulets and talismans from elements believed to hold protective powers—stones, herbs, metals—to serve as barriers against malevolent forces. Adorn your abode with protective symbols; inscribe runes and sigils upon your thresholds as bastions against misfortune. In ancient traditions, iron placed above doorways and rowan trees planted near homes stood as venerable defenses against curses cast by envious hearts.

"Embrace these age-old practices, keeper of hushed hexes, and may your journey be free from the shadow of Ötzi's curse and the malice of restless spirits."

Ötzi's Curse

JUNE 1991, ÖTZTAL ALPS, AUSTRIAN-ITALIAN BORDER

In the shadow of the Ötztal Alps, Tobias stumbled upon a sight that would mark both a remarkable discovery and the beginning of his own end. Protruding from a glacier's icy grip was a figure—a man preserved by time. Tobias's heart raced with excitement and awe; he had found a buried iceman.

The iceman's skin was leathery and browned by millennia in the glacier's clutches. Though worn by time, his face bore an expression of eternal rest, and his attire was of another age: woven grasses and animal hides that spoke of a life tied intimately to nature.

Tobias's heart thrummed with excitement and reverence. Yet as he extended a trembling hand toward this messenger from antiquity, a chill that transcended the cold mountain air coursed through him.

Heeding this silent warning, Tobias withdrew his hand. A profound respect for the iceman's eternal slumber washed over him. He chose to leave the discovery untouched, allowing Ötzi to remain ensconced in his frozen tomb.

And so, Tobias departed, but not before his gaze fell upon a small, intricately carved amulet lying near the iceman's resting place. With a hesitant hand, Tobias picked up the amulet, feeling its weight and the coldness of its stone.

As he pocketed the artifact, Tobias felt a twinge of guilt for disturbing the sanctity of Ötzi's tomb. Yet, he couldn't help but feel drawn to this token, as if it were meant for him.

Carrying this small piece, Tobias came down from the alpine heights, unaware that this memento would soon become a harbinger of his fate.

Days later, Tobias's elation turned to tragedy. The night was draped in a shroud of darkness as he drove through the winding roads that cut through the heart of the Alps.

Tobias's hands were steady on the wheel, his mind occupied with thoughts of the ancient iceman. But as he drove, an unsettling feeling crept over him: a sense that he was not alone on this desolate stretch of road.

A sudden chill swept through the car, and Tobias's eyes flicked to the rearview mirror. For a moment, he saw it—a dark figure seated in the back. He blinked, and the figure was gone, but the feeling of dread lingered.

The road ahead twisted like a serpent. Tobias's focus returned to the path before him, but the darkness was not done with him yet. It swirled outside the car, a tangible force that clawed at the edges of his sanity. The wind howled, a mournful cry that echoed the iceman's anguish, and with it came a whisper, a voice from the depths of time, speaking a language long forgotten.

"Give it back," it hissed, a command more felt than heard.

Tobias's pulse thundered in his ears. The car's headlights flickered, and the figure appeared again in that brief moment of darkness, this time on the road ahead. Tobias's grip tightened on the steering wheel, his knuckles pale as he fought to maintain control.

With a desperate twist, Tobias tried to avoid the apparition, but it was too late. The car spun, a dance with death as the figure loomed ever closer. The world turned upside down, and Tobias's last thought was of the iceman who had reached across time to claim what was his.

The Golden Pharaoh's Legacy: Unveiling Tutankhamun's Tomb and the Curse Myth

Pharaoh Tutankhamun, or King Tut, ruled over ancient Egypt in the 1300s BCE. His tomb was unearthed in 1922 by British archaeologist Howard Carter and financier Lord Carnarvon. The tomb's remarkable state of preservation was a notable aspect of the discovery.

Within the tomb, a treasure trove of artifacts was discovered, all intended to accompany the pharaoh into the afterlife. But alongside the discovery of Tutankhamun's tomb arose stories of a curse that would afflict anyone who disturbed the pharaoh's rest. This idea was fueled by the deaths of several people connected to the tomb's discovery, including Lord Carnarvon. Media sensationalism attributed these deaths to the "curse of Tutankhamun," suggesting that an inscription in the tomb pronounced death upon those who disturbed it.

The Baubas's Hideaway
THE STELMUŽĖ OAK TREE

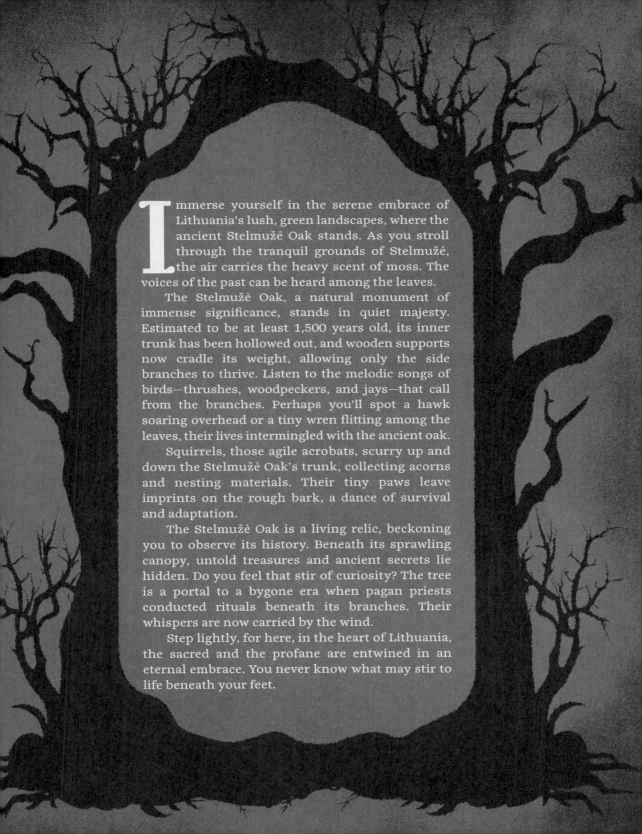

Immerse yourself in the serene embrace of Lithuania's lush, green landscapes, where the ancient Stelmužė Oak stands. As you stroll through the tranquil grounds of Stelmužė, the air carries the heavy scent of moss. The voices of the past can be heard among the leaves.

The Stelmužė Oak, a natural monument of immense significance, stands in quiet majesty. Estimated to be at least 1,500 years old, its inner trunk has been hollowed out, and wooden supports now cradle its weight, allowing only the side branches to thrive. Listen to the melodic songs of birds—thrushes, woodpeckers, and jays—that call from the branches. Perhaps you'll spot a hawk soaring overhead or a tiny wren flitting among the leaves, their lives intermingled with the ancient oak.

Squirrels, those agile acrobats, scurry up and down the Stelmužė Oak's trunk, collecting acorns and nesting materials. Their tiny paws leave imprints on the rough bark, a dance of survival and adaptation.

The Stelmužė Oak is a living relic, beckoning you to observe its history. Beneath its sprawling canopy, untold treasures and ancient secrets lie hidden. Do you feel that stir of curiosity? The tree is a portal to a bygone era when pagan priests conducted rituals beneath its branches. Their whispers are now carried by the wind.

Step lightly, for here, in the heart of Lithuania, the sacred and the profane are entwined in an eternal embrace. You never know what may stir to life beneath your feet.

Y ou brace yourself against the tree's immense girth, a wonder of nature that has seen empires rise and fall. The Stelmužė Oak is a chronicler of stories and it shares its tale in a voice that rumbles from deep within its core. "The Baubas," it intones, "is not just a fright for misbehaving children. It is the darkness in the corner of your eye, the discomfort that creeps into your soul, the crux of caution chanted through the ages. Something wicked this way comes.

"In the quiet of the night, in the liminal space where reality and nightmare blur, the Baubas stirs. This crafty demon skulks in the ancient lands of Lithuania. A fixture in the nocturnal imaginations of the Baltic people, the Baubas is known to hide in the unwatched nooks of your home and wait for the perfect moment to terrify.

"The Baubas thrives in darkness and is steeped in Lithuania's age-old traditions. It is a legacy of stories told by firelight, tales that have seeped into the land's old bones. This figure embodies ancestral fears by representing a dark reflection of dread that lingers deep in the heart of humanity.

"Before Christianization, Lithuanians practiced polytheism—the worship of many gods. Their beliefs were transmitted orally through generations without written texts or religious books. The earliest insights into Lithuanian mythology were not from the Lithuanians themselves but from the observations of travelers, missionaries, and historians.

"Romuva, the ancient Lithuanian faith, was the last pagan religion to persist in Europe. Lithuania officially converted to Christianity in 1387, primarily for political reasons. Despite the adoption of Christianity, the resilience of the pre-Christian Lithuanian religion is evident. Many deities transformed into Christian saints, allowing for their continued worship. This persistence is further seen in the survival of elements of Lithuanian mythology in folklore, customs, and festive rituals that highlight the enduring nature of cultural beliefs.

"Over time, once-holy deities have been reduced to mythological animals or natural forces in subsequent folktales. Lithuanian mythology transitioned from oral tradition to survival in customs and folklore, maintaining its unique blend of ancient beliefs and Christian influences.

"Within these beliefs the Baubas is a creature of contradiction. Small yet oddly stretched, with limbs elongated like a spider, it folds itself into corners so snugly that one would never know it's there. Its form blends into the domestic landscape seamlessly, appearing as a natural, albeit sinister, part of your home's architecture. Where hearth fires flicker and night's breath fogs the glass, the Baubas bides its time. A being of whimsy and spite, it is a phantom that stalks the quiet moments before dreams take hold.

Similar Creatures in Folklore

Bogeyman
ANGLOSPHERE

A shadowy figure, usually with claws, horns, or sharp fangs, that lurks in closets or beneath beds.

Butzemann/Busemann
GERMANY

The Butzemann is a straw man that scares children in the fields, while the Busemann is a dark figure with a hat and coat that lurks in the shadows.

Coco/Cuco
HISPANOSPHERE

A monster that consumes children who disobey their parents or don't go to sleep on time. Its appearance is varied, though it is often depicted as a shadowy figure, lurking in dark corners and under beds.

Bubák
CZECH REPUBLIC

In some stories, the Bubák resembles a scarecrow. Another depiction presents the Bubák as an elderly man carrying a big sack on his back. It hops around during the night, looking for prey.

Babau
ITALY

A bogeyman that takes children away at night if they do not go to sleep.

Hans Trapp
FRANCE

A legendary figure who visits children before Christmas, dressed as a scarecrow, and scares those who have misbehaved.

El Coco
PORTUGAL

Similar to the Spanish Cuco, a monster that preys on misbehaving children.

El Hombre Del Saco
SPAIN

A man who carries a sack and takes away children who misbehave.

Guschg Herdsmen's Doll
LIECHTENSTEIN

A figure used by herdsmen to scare children away from the dangers of the Alps.

"The Baubas melds into the crevices of existence. It is an entity of stealth and cunning. Its shape is so deeply entwined with the homely milieu that its presence might not be discerned until the sun goes down. It is a flicker in your peripheral vision and a shadow where none should be cast. This is the Baubas, unfurling from its hiding place with creased limbs and eyes aflame with malevolent glee. It thrives in the craft of trepidation.

"The Baubas manipulates darkness as it stretches and contorts into terrifying shapes that dance on the walls, growing ever more ominous with each glimmer of light. It may animate the inanimate, making objects appear alive briefly to cultivate an atmosphere of dread before the lights come on.

"Born from the communal fear of the unseen, it is the quintessence of admonitory fables and an omnipresent specter in the musings of naughty children. For the children of Lithuania, the Baubas is the bogeyman, the facilitator of discipline. 'Mind your ways, or the Baubas shall fetch you,' parents warn, summoning the name of the dusky trickster to coax compliance. In Lithuanian lore, the Baubas endures as a symbol of fear and the power of parental guidance to mold the young.

"The story of the Baubas most likely comes from a more primitive, older belief that has been transformed over time into a folktale creature meant to instill fear and obedience. It acts as the personification of cautionary stories, a constant presence that looms large in the minds of children who misbehave.

"The impenetrable forests and relentless grip of Lithuanian winters have undoubtedly influenced the conception of the Baubas. In the collective imagination, these environments give rise to phantoms and entities that embody the mystery and menace of the natural world.

"In many civilizations, the bogeyman embodies terror, a creature of the night that preys on children. This concept transcends borders, with each country having its own version of this cautionary figure. From the Babau of Italy to the Almas of Mongolia, the bogeyman is a global pantheon, reflecting each place's unique fears, societal norms, and community ethics. It has no fixed appearance, allowing it to adapt to the cultural context of each society. The widespread existence of bogeyman figures suggests a deep-rooted psychological mechanism that transcends cultural boundaries.

"To protect oneself from the Baubas, one must keep their home well-lit and free of dark corners where it might hide. It is also wise to maintain a tidy space, as clutter provides the Baubas with ample hiding spots. Above all, one should carry a brave heart, for the Baubas feed on fear, and courage can banish it back to the darkness from where it came.

"Bearer of mirth and light, in the dance of shadows where the Baubas stalks, let these ancient remedies be your fortress and behave yourself. Fill thy dwelling with the resonance of laughter, for joy is a bane to the Baubas's gloom. As day resigns itself to night, let a lamp's gentle glow persist, a beacon to cast the Baubas into the netherworld's embrace.

"Embrace these practices, heralder of cheer, and may your home be a bright and merry haven untouched by the Baubas's somber reach.

"So, my friend, as you lay in your bed and the night deepens, remember the Baubas. It is the whisper in the silence, the chill down your spine, and the keeper of ancient warnings."

Do You Know Why I Come?

JULY 1988, PLATELIAI, LITHUANIA

In the Lithuanian village of Plateliai, two sisters, Natalie and Ava, traveled with their mother to meet her new boyfriend and stay at the vacation home his family owned near a beautiful lake. But the tension quickly grew as the girls were unsure how to interact with this newcomer. It had only been a year since their parents' divorce, and they felt disloyal to their father.

Minor disputes arose and they ridiculed their mother's new boyfriend and giggled behind his back when their mother was out of earshot. They told themselves that they didn't care whether he heard, and from the looks of hurt that would flash across his face at these not-so-secret jibes, he had. But he said nothing. As the day went on, sometimes Natalie and Ava each inwardly felt something a little like guilt prick her conscience, but each girl tried her best to ignore it.

Settling in for their first night, Natalie and Ava moved through their bedtime routines with quiet efficiency. Each was lost in thought about the man who had so subtly altered their family dynamic.

The night closed in, and the sisters drifted into an uneasy sleep.

Natalie was the first to stir, her eyes fluttering open. At the foot of her bed stood an entity. Its form was twisted and stretched, with long limbs unfurling. Its eyes glinted with malevolence.

"Natalie . . ." the voice slithered through the darkness. "*Natalllllie . . .*" it hissed again, drawing out her name like a blade across the tongue.

With trembling fingers, she reached out for the switch. The room flooded with warm light, banishing shadows. The entity wailed and dissipated.

Ava was roused by a cold breeze as the entity attempted to lift her mattress. She giggled at first, thinking it was a prank. But as the entity's intentions became clear, Ava's fearlessness transformed into fiery courage. "Get outta here!" she screamed. Unaccustomed to such bravery from its young victims, the creature faltered and faded away into nothingness.

The following day, the sisters shuffled into the cozy kitchen, their faces evident with exhaustion and fear. Their mother, a kindhearted woman with a hint of weariness in her eyes, sat at the head of the table. Beside her was her boyfriend, who looked equally somber.

Natalie and Ava exchanged glances that weighed heavily with a secret unknowingly shared.

Their mother poured tea, her gaze moving from one daughter to another. "You all seem quiet this morning," she said gently. "Did something happen?"

Natalie hesitated. "Last night, I saw something," she began. "A monster. It stood at the foot of my bed."

Ava interrupted, her voice small. "It tried to lift my mattress."

Their mother's boyfriend shifted in his chair. "When I was your age, the Baubas visited me too."

"What is this 'Baubas'?" their mother asked.

The man's gaze met Natalie's. "A bogeyman creature."

Their mother's eyes softened. "We'll protect each other," she said. And she gave her boyfriend a sly wink. And so, they forged an unspoken pact over breakfast to face the Baubas—together.

The Seven O'Clock Man's Silent Hunt

The story of the Seven O'Clock Man is a French-Canadian legend that warns children to go to bed before 7 p.m., or else they will be taken away by a mysterious figure who roams the streets at night.

Every night, when the clock strikes seven, an entity creeps out of the alleys and corners of the city. He wears a long cloak and a wide-brimmed hat that obscures his face. He carries a large sack, big enough to fit a child. He is the Seven O'Clock Man, looking for his next victim.

He walks silently, listening for any sound of disobedience. He can hear the whispers of children who are still awake, playing games, reading books, or watching TV. He can smell their fear and excitement. He knows where they live and he knows how to get in. He can pick any lock, climb any window, or slip through any crack. He is unstoppable.

The Huaka'i Pō's Path

THE 'ŌHI'A LEHUA TREE

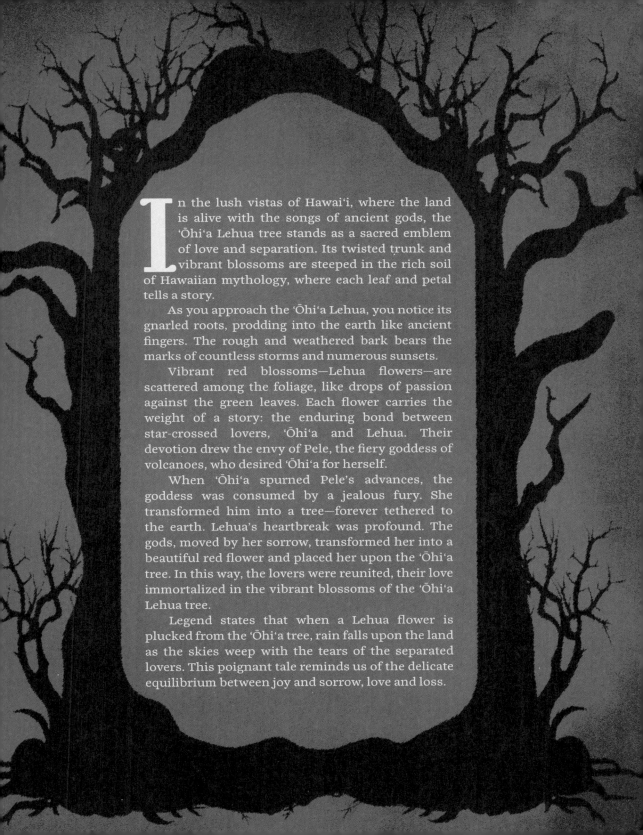

In the lush vistas of Hawai'i, where the land is alive with the songs of ancient gods, the 'Ōhi'a Lehua tree stands as a sacred emblem of love and separation. Its twisted trunk and vibrant blossoms are steeped in the rich soil of Hawaiian mythology, where each leaf and petal tells a story.

As you approach the 'Ōhi'a Lehua, you notice its gnarled roots, prodding into the earth like ancient fingers. The rough and weathered bark bears the marks of countless storms and numerous sunsets.

Vibrant red blossoms—Lehua flowers—are scattered among the foliage, like drops of passion against the green leaves. Each flower carries the weight of a story: the enduring bond between star-crossed lovers, 'Ōhi'a and Lehua. Their devotion drew the envy of Pele, the fiery goddess of volcanoes, who desired 'Ōhi'a for herself.

When 'Ōhi'a spurned Pele's advances, the goddess was consumed by a jealous fury. She transformed him into a tree—forever tethered to the earth. Lehua's heartbreak was profound. The gods, moved by her sorrow, transformed her into a beautiful red flower and placed her upon the 'Ōhi'a tree. In this way, the lovers were reunited, their love immortalized in the vibrant blossoms of the 'Ōhi'a Lehua tree.

Legend states that when a Lehua flower is plucked from the 'Ōhi'a tree, rain falls upon the land as the skies weep with the tears of the separated lovers. This poignant tale reminds us of the delicate equilibrium between joy and sorrow, love and loss.

Υou stand beneath the ʻŌhiʻa Lehua, its vibrant red blossoms a stark reminder of enduring love and the fiery temper of Pele. The tree, rooted deeply in the rich volcanic soil, shares its tale in a voice that echoes the heartbeat of the islands. "The Night Marchers," it speaks, "are not mere phantoms. They are the guardians of these lands, the protectors of sacred traditions, and the embodiment of a warrior's eternal commitment."

"On the darkened paths of Hawaiian lore, amalgamated with the threads of myth and the hues of ancestral memory, Huakaʻi Pō—the Night Marchers—advance through the gloaming. These spectral processions, known as ʻoiʻo, are the echoes of ancient dignitaries, their phantom footsteps a hallowed cadence in the stillness of the islands. They are a ghostly fleet of warriors, the phantoms of death that stride to the rhythm of their own beat.

"The Huakaʻi Pō are no benign spirits; they are the vengeful souls of warriors, chiefs, and gods bound to the mortal realm by the sacred rites of kapu, the ancient laws governing the sacred and the profane. Their eyes, hollow and unseeing, blaze with the fires of the afterlife, a ghastly glow that illuminates the well-worn paths. They march in lockstep, a procession of doom that leaves no trace but a terror that lingers.

"Their faces are twisted in eternal rage, their cloaks stained with the blood of battles long forgotten. They carry the scent of decay, a miasma of death that clings to the air as a malevolent fog. As they march, they are shrouded in the glow of kukui torches, their light piercing through rain and darkness. Whirlwinds trail in their wake, and the cry of ʻKapu o moe!ʼ is a dire warning to all to honor the sacred procession. The march of the gods is a spectacle of reverence, their path illuminated by crimson torches, accompanied by the elemental chorus of rain, thunder, and the tumultuous sea.

"The ground trembles beneath their ghostly feet, and the wind carries their mournful cries, a lamentation for the lives they once led. The Huakaʻi Pō are relentless, their path determined, a route carved by the hands of fate. They traverse the land with a purpose that is as inexorable as the tides, their passage a grim reminder of the power of the ancient Hawaiian gods.

"The Huakaʻi Pō are the revered spirits of chiefs and warriors and the gods themselves, each with their own sacred march. In times past, the living processions of Hawaiian nobility were grand affairs heralded by a voice commanding respect and submission. The highest of ranks demanded prostration, while others merited a respectful squat. The most divine were carried aloft, their feet never sullying the earth, their passage a sanctified event. Such rites are observed for the spectral warriors of the night march.

Similar Creatures in Folklore

Wild Hunt (page 106)
EUROPE

A group of ghostly hunters passing in wild pursuit, often seen as an omen of catastrophe or death.

Sluagh
IRELAND AND SCOTLAND

Restless spirits of the sinful dead, sometimes seen flying in groups through the skies in a collective movement.

Procession of the Dead
GLOBAL

Tales of spectral processions that travel through specific routes, often associated with specific times of the year or certain conditions.

Ghostly Armies
GLOBAL

Legends of phantom armies seen marching or battling.

Ankou (page 173)
BRITTANY, FRANCE

A personification of death that travels in a creaking cart or leads a procession.

"At the vanguard of these ghostly parades strides the alo kapu, the chief of sacred face, while the akua kapu, the chief of hallowed back, brings up the rear. Between them march the ghostly warriors, a guard for those shielded in life. To cross paths with the Huakaʻi Pō is to encounter the spirit of kapu.

"The Huakaʻi Pō march through the islands, their path unyielding, their route unwavering. They traverse the modern world, indifferent to the barriers of stone and steel. Their journey is one of tradition. They march to the beat of drums and the whisper of nose flutes and other instruments, or simply in ominous silence, reflecting the preferences of the chief they once served.

"The Huakaʻi Pō parade on nights dictated by the lunar calendar. Their presence is most potent when the moon wanes or renews. They are the guardians of the spirit, their procession a solemn escort to the afterworld. They celebrate at heiau and familiar gathering grounds, their attire unchanged from the life they once knew.

"To cross the path of the night marchers is to invite terror. The naïve who find themselves in the presence of the Huakaʻi Pō must prostrate themselves lest they incur the wrath of these formidable specters. It is said that only the intervention of an ʻaumakua, an ancestral guardian spirit, can spare one from a fate worse than death.

"The Night Marchers embody primordial terror, a force that demands respect and fear in equal measure. They are the keepers of the night, the guardians of the threshold between life and death. In their march, they carry the burden of history, a legacy of power and retribution reverberating through the ages.

"The Night Marchers, thought to be the phantoms of ancient Hawaiian warriors, reflect the islands' intricate caste system and the deep reverence held for the aliʻi, the noble chiefs. They are the echoes of a society that revered its leaders, their spirits still marching in eternal homage to the traditions of old.

"The dramatic geography of Hawaiʻi, with its fiery volcanoes and the vast ocean's embrace, influences the lore of the Night Marchers. They are envisioned rising from the sea's depths or descending the mountain slopes, their ghostly ranks a mirror to the land's majestic and formidable nature.

"In Hawaiian belief, where kapu govern the balance of the spiritual and the earthly, the Night Marchers enforce these ancient laws. Their march is a solemn reminder of the importance of respect and the dire consequences that befall those who dare to transgress these sacred norms.

"Historical events, too, have dictated the Night Marchers' narrative. They are said to march in honor of Hawaiian gods or toward hallowed sites, their spectral journey perhaps tied to the great battles of the past or the preservation of Hawaiian customs and traditions.

"At the core of the Night Marchers' tales lies the universal human confrontation with mortality and the unknown. The reverence for ancestors and the primal fear of death imbue these stories with a resonant psychological depth.

"Voyager of the sacred isles, when the Huakaʻi Pō march beneath the moon's mute gaze, heed these edicts born of the ancients: Let not your presence disrupt their solemn parade, for to cross the path of the Night Marchers is to court the shadows' deepest frown. If the thrum of drums or the flicker of torchlight reaches you, withdraw; seek not the company of this spectral host.

"If in their midst, make the earth your bed, curl as the unborn, and show your reverence for the warriors and the land: Such humility may grant you mercy. Avert your eyes, for in the Night Marchers' gaze lies a fate most dire, a curse that whispers of oblivion. If your blood sings with the call of the islands, if the Night Marchers are kin of your kin, then their march shall pass you by, a ghostly benediction.

"Let these words be your guide, sojourner of the starlit paths, and may the march, the eternal vigil of the ancients, leave you untouched.

"So, it is with the Huaka'i Pō, the Night Marchers of Hawai'i, a legacy of reverence and respect. Their march is not just a procession but a walk between the worlds, a connection between the living and the ancestors. It is a reminder of the sacred cycles that govern life and death. In the hush of evening, when the sky darkens, and the stars emerge, remember the Huaka'i Pō, for their march is the heartbeat of the islands, a rhythm that resonates with the soul of Hawai'i."

They Don't Like Being Watched

APRIL 2012, HONOLULU, HAWAI'I, UNITED STATES

It was a moonless night, and Alelo, a security guard at the Davies Pacific Center in Honolulu, sat in his dimly lit office on the twenty-third floor. The building hummed with the usual sounds, but then the monitors flickered, and Alelo's attention snapped to the security feed.

His eyes remained fixed on the screen as ghostly forms appeared, moving with purpose, their outlines flickering in the dim light. He squinted, trying to decipher their features.

The room grew colder as the spectral figures advanced. Their skin clung to their bones like tattered rags. Hollow eyes stared out from sunken sockets, devoid of any humanity. Their limbs moved with unnatural precision as they marched in tandem. Alelo's breath caught in his throat. These were not mere apparitions. They were something older, darker, and far more malevolent.

His pragmatic mind raced, seeking rational explanations.

He stopped and rewound the footage, studying the figures' movements as his trembling fingers dialed the extension of his manager, Kai. The phone rang, each chime drawn out. When Kai's voice crackled through the receiver, Alelo hesitated. How could he explain what he saw? How could he ask for help without sounding insane?

"Kai," Alelo began, his voice steady despite his inner turmoil. "Something's happening on the monitors. I need you to come up to the twenty-third floor."

Kai sounded concerned. "What is it?"

Alelo glanced back at the screens. The footage replayed the ghostly figures' silent procession. "I'm not sure," he responded.

A few minutes later Kai arrived, flashlight in hand. He squinted at the screen, his coffee-stained uniform bringing an element of normalcy to the drama unfolding. "What are they?" Alelo asked, pointing at the flickering figures.

Kai scratched his grizzled beard. "Night Marchers—Huaka'i Pō," he said matter-of-factly. "Ancient protectors. They walk the old paths, guarding what's sacred."

Alelo's skepticism flared. "You believe in this?"

Kai leaned closer. "Seen 'em myself. Late nights when the air gets thick. They're restless souls, bound by duty."

"But why here?" Alelo gestured at the screen. "In our office building?"

Kai's eyes held ancient wisdom. "The Davies Pacific Center stands on their trail. They march through time. Maybe they seek justice or vengeance. Or maybe they're warning us."

Alelo's logical mind rebelled. "This is absurd."

Kai shrugged. "Absurd or not, they're real. And they don't like being watched."

As if on cue, the monitors glitched again. The Night Marchers vanished, leaving only static.

Guardians of the Islands: The Sacred Ti Plant and Hawaiian Salt

Ti and Hawaiian salt are integral to Hawaiian culture for their spiritual properties. The ti plant, sacred to the gods Lono and Laka, has leaves used in leis (traditional Hawaiian garlands or wreaths), hula skirts, and necklaces. Hawaiian salt, known for its cleansing abilities, removes impurities and negative energy.

Both are believed to protect from harm and attract blessings. People plant ti around homes, wear ti leis, or carry ti leaves for good luck. Hawaiian salt is sprinkled around doors, windows, and beds, or used to cleanse crystals, jewelry, and tools.

The Grim Reaper, the Final Voyage

THE YEW TREE

Amid the sacred silence of the ancient graveyard, the air hangs heavy with the scent of damp earth and memories long buried. The entrance is marked by an iron gate that creaks as it swings open, enticing you to step across the threshold. The path, worn smooth by countless footsteps, winds through a maze of lichen-covered tombstones.

To your left is a weathered angel—a marble figure with wings outstretched in sublimation, its face engraved with sorrow. Ahead, a row of Celtic crosses leans slightly. Their intricate carvings tell stories of lives lived and lost as moss clings to them, a delicate pattern of decay. To your right, a family plot lies sheltered beneath the Yew tree's ancient branches. The gnarled roots submerge around the graves, their grip disturbing the earth. Names and dates are inscribed into the headstones, some barely legible, others worn smooth by time's unrelenting touch. Though they may never have met one another, generations rest side by side, their stories interwoven.

The Yew's presence in churchyards is also considered practical; its roots were believed to keep the dead in place, and its dense foliage provided shelter from the elements for parishioners attending church. Yet in some areas, it was feared that Yews sheltered witches, and people were advised to avoid the trees.

And so, with each step, you honor the past—the forgotten, the cherished, the nameless.

Y ou stand beneath the Yew, its branches arching like the vaults of a cathedral. With its toxic needles and enduring wood, the Yew shares its tale in a voice as deep as the roots that anchor it to the earth. "The Reaper," it speaks. "He is the final harvest, the severance of life, the collector of souls.

"The Grim Reaper emerged in the shadows of medieval Europe. A personification of death itself, he is often imagined as a hooded skeleton wielding a scythe, a tool used traditionally for reaping crops. The scythe now repurposed for harvesting souls, the Reaper performs his solemn duty.

"This imagery became associated with death during the fourteenth century, coinciding with the devastating Black Death pandemic. His scythe came to represent the cutting down of life in its prime, much like how the plague took lives indiscriminately. The widespread death and suffering caused by the plague led to a personification of death in a way that was understandable to the people of that time.

"The Reaper's gaze is empty yet all-seeing, peering from beneath his cowl with an unspoken understanding of fate's final decree. His skeletal hands, firm and unwavering, grip the scythe with an eternal resolve. His cloak blends with the encroaching darkness. Those who encounter him find not malice, but inevitability.

"The Grim Reaper is a graphic reminder of mortality, serving as a memento mori—a Latin phrase meaning 'remember you must die'—a common theme in art and literature during and after the plague era. It reminded people that death is inevitable and impartial, coming for all regardless of status or wealth.

"The imagery of a being coming to escort souls to the afterlife can be traced back to earlier mythologies and religions where psychopomps were common. What is a psychopomp, you ask? The term 'psychopomp'—originating from the Greek words 'psyche' meaning 'soul' and 'pompe' meaning 'guide' or 'conductor'—is attributed to those figures who fulfill this sacred role of guiding the deceased, ensuring their safe passage to the afterlife.

"Greek mythology frequently portrays Hermes, the gods' messenger, as a psychopomp. With his winged sandals and caduceus, he guides spirits to the underworld, where they will ultimately find peace. This role is not unique to Hermes; many cultures harbor their own versions of psychopomps, each with distinct attributes but united in purpose.

"Psychopomps serve as emblems of transition, embodying both an end and a beginning. They navigate the liminal spaces between worlds and states of being, offering guidance to souls embarking on their most profound journey.

Similar Creatures in Folklore

Santa Muerte

MEXICO

A female folk saint or goddess of death, often represented as a skeleton.

Shinigami

JAPAN

Spirits or gods who, in Japanese folklore, invite people to die.

Ankou (page 165)

BRITTANY, FRANCE

A figure who gathers the spirits of the dead, frequently shown as a skeleton or man with a cloak on and a scythe in hand.

The Morrigan

IRELAND

Sometimes associated with death and fate, particularly in the form of a crow or raven.

La Parca

SPAIN

A figure similar to the Grim Reaper, often depicted as a skeletal being who comes to collect the souls of the dead.

Mavka

UKRAINE

Spirits of young women who died untimely deaths and are associated with death and the afterlife.

Giltinė

LITHUANIA

The personification of death, often depicted as an old, ugly woman with a long, poisonous tongue.

"The Grim Reaper, cloaked in shadow and wielding a scythe, is one of the most recognizable psychopomps in Western culture. This spectral entity is a symbolic figure that has evolved over centuries, drawing from various cultural influences, including Charon, the ferryman of Hades in Greek mythology, and the Angel of Death found in multiple religious texts.

"As a psychopomp, the Grim Reaper's role transcends mere symbolism; it represents the inexorable nature of death and the certainty of life's end. The Reaper's scythe cuts through the metaphysical tether binding the soul to the body, while its skeletal visage is a stark reminder of your own mortality.

"This figure's presence in art, literature, and folklore has cemented its status as an enduring psychopomp. The Grim Reaper's portrayal varies from a silent guide who arrives at the predetermined moment to a more interactive presence that might offer last words or comfort to those about to embark on their final voyage. Regardless of its depiction, the Grim Reaper remains a potent symbol of life's final transition and the ultimate psychopomp guiding humanity through the veil of death.

"Traveler, understand that the Grim Reaper's visitation is a certainty that no precaution or safeguard can deter. This solemn harbinger arrives at the appointed hour, impartial to rank or riches, to guide each soul to its final destination. The Reaper's presence is a reminder of your shared destiny and the universal truth that life's journey must one day end.

"In this knowledge, there is wisdom: to cherish each moment, to forge bonds of love and kinship, and to live a life that will be remembered. As you walk your path, do so with the courage and grace that will define your legacy—a legacy that endures beyond the Reaper's silent call."

The Helping Hand

NOVEMBER 2023, VIRGINIA, UNITED STATES

Nurse Alice's story is one of quiet determination and boundless empathy. In the hallowed halls of a hospice called Edenbrook Haven, she is more than a caregiver; she is a listener of legacies, a tender guardian of the fading embers of memory.

As Nurse Alice's shift stretched into the night, the witching hour was upon her. Alice's heart raced as she felt the change, the atmosphere dense with a chilling anticipation. The routine check became a somber clicking through the endless night.

Her call to a friend was intended as a lifeline to normalcy, but it became a desperate plea whispered into the receiver. The laughter and conversation, meant to be a balm, instead seemed to mock her growing unease. Then she noticed Mrs. Winters, the frail woman whose life was ebbing away with each labored breath.

The darkness in the room deepened, coalescing into a form beside the old woman's bed. An impossibly white, cold, skeletal hand emerged from the shadows, its touch not of this world. It hovered over Mrs. Winters's face. The monitors began to flicker, and the heartbeats of both women stuttered—one was fixed to a machine and the other stood observing.

Alice watched as the hand seemed to beckon, calling forth the essence of Mrs. Winters. Alice's breath hitched as her eyes fixated on the spectral hand that emerged from the shadows. The fingers, elongated and skeletal, curled slowly, deliberately, as if welcoming into the gloom.

The hand beckoned with a motion that appeared to distort the air around it. Each curl of the finger was a silent command, a sinister invitation that Alice felt deep in her bones. The essence of Mrs. Winters seemed to be drawn out, inch by chilling inch, toward the hand that claimed her from beyond the grave.

Alice's voice faltered mid-sentence. "I . . . I have to call you back," she stammered, ending the call to her friend.

She approached Mrs. Winters's bedside, her steps hesitant, her mind reeling with disbelief. The room was as it should be, save for the lingering chill that seemed to cling to the air. No one was there—no sign of the hand, but it had seemed so real, so intent. She pulled the blankets up around Mrs. Winters's sleeping form and left the room.

The night passed, each tick of the clock reminding her of what she had witnessed. As dawn broke, Alice's shift ended and she found herself driving home, the weight of her encounter heavy on her shoulders.

"What if it was the Grim Reaper that I saw?" she pondered. The question slipped from her lips and into the emptiness of her car's interior.

The thought consumed her, a seed of dread that took root and grew with every passing mile. If it had been the Reaper, then surely Mrs. Winters . . .

The next day, with a heart laden with apprehension, Alice returned to the ward. She made her way to Mrs. Winters's room and there, in the bed where the old woman had lain, was nothing but rumpled sheets and the residue of a life that once was. Mrs. Winters had passed. Her journey on this earth concluded in the quiet hours of the morning.

Global Mortuary Rites: A Glimpse into Cultural Ceremonies of Death

Death practices represent each culture's unique relationship with mortality, embodying beliefs about the afterlife, the soul's journey, and the community's role in honoring the deceased. Here are a few examples.

Famadihana: In Madagascar, this "turning of the bones" ritual involves exhuming the dead, rewrapping them in fresh burial clothes, and dancing with the wrapped bodies to music. This is believed to speed up decomposition and help the spirit to cross over to the afterlife.

Water Burial: Some Nordic cultures use water as a burial ground, setting bodies adrift in death ships on rivers or the ocean to return them to the gods or the revered water.

The Parade: In Varanasi, India, the dead are paraded through the streets, dressed in colors representing their virtues, and sprinkled with water from the Ganges River before the cremation to encourage souls to reach salvation.

Conclusion

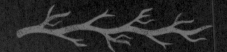

As the wildwood's embrace recedes and the moon's argent farewell graces your journey, ponder the imprints left by distant shores and fervent beliefs upon these ancient tales. The wildwood whispers stories tinged with the remnants of colonization and the zealous hymns of new religions. These external powers, seeking dominion over land and spirit, forever alter and evolve the essence of folklore.

Yet, within these stories lies a resilience, a steadfast grip on the roots that anchor these legends to their true nature. Though shaped by conquest and creed, the wildwood's lore retains its wild heart, evidence of the enduring power of stories to withstand the tides of change.

Environmental changes, too, can shape folklore, as natural events like floods, droughts, or celestial occurrences often become a part of the stories. But let's not overlook the true defenders of folklore: the storytellers. They are the ones who breathe life into lore with unique interpretations and flair, adding their own nuance and imagination while inspiring all.

Language is a powerful vessel, carrying stories across generations and borders, sometimes altering them in translation. Political upheavals and social movements also leave their mark, as stories often reflect the peoples' struggles and aspirations. The spirit of folklore culminates in a shared human experience, promoting a sense of connection and belonging.

So, as you traverse the world beyond these hallowed groves, let the wildwood's ancient wisdom guide you through life. May you find solace in knowing that despite the shadows cast by an ever-changing world, the spirit of folklore endures evergreen and eternal. And remember, though the faces and places may evolve, the essence of your struggles and triumphs remains constant.

Your ancestors' tales are not so different from your own—they, too, danced with change yet stood firm in the face of it, just as you must do now.

Carry these stories with you, like embers from a sacred fire, and let them illuminate the corners of your mind. Be watchful, for the world is a symphony of wonders and whispers, each seeking the attentive soul. Let the wildwood's wisdom be your guide, opening your eyes to the unseen, to the mysteries that dance in the periphery of perception.

And when the mundane threatens to blacken your vision, remember the enchantment of the wildwood. It beckons you to return, to wander once more through its verdant vaults and discover anew the stories that breathe life into the old bark and stone.

So, farewell, for now, brave voyager of the veiled vales. Keep the wildwood's secrets close and its lessons closer. In your journey through the world, you will find that the wildwood never truly leaves you—it resides within, a constant companion, whispering of the beauty in the beast, the light in the darkness, and the truth in the tale.

Return soon, for the wildwood awaits. Its stories are a never-ending wellspring of discovery.

References

Árnadóttir, Nanna. "Record Number of Reports of Missing Children." *The Reykavík Grapevine*. Published April 13, 2017. grapevine.is/news/2017/04/13/missing-children.

Bridges, Will, dir. *Paranormal Witness*. Season 3, episode 9, "The Wolf Pack." Written by Will Bridges. Aired August 7, 2013, on Syfy.

Briggs, Stacia. "Weird Norfolk: Black Shuck Sighting at Gorleston, April 1972." *Eastern Daily Press*. Published May 12, 2017. www.edp24.co.uk/news/20837578. weird-norfolk-black-shuck-sighting-gorleston-april-1972.

Cecco, Leyland. "Sasquatch or Wendigo? Mysterious Howls in Canadian Wilderness Spark Confusion." *The Guardian*. Published November 15, 2019. www.theguardian. com/world/2019/nov/15/canada-forest-howls-shrieks-video.

Charleston, LJ. "The Frightening Supernatural Story of the Black Bird of Chernobyl." Published June 15, 2019. www.news.com.au/technology/ environment/the-frightening-supernatural-story-of-the-black-bird-of-chernobyl/ news-story/74ea2f417564e6ca1a289e0813d09341.

Creed, Barbara. *The Monstrous-Feminine: Film, Feminism, Psychoanalysis*, 1st ed. London: Routledge, 1993.

Deutsche Welle. "'Curse of the Iceman' Linked to Scientist's Death." Published June 11, 2005. www.dw.com/en/curse-of-the-iceman-linked-to-scientists-death/a-1765550.

Kastenbaum, Robert. "Sudden Unexpected Nocturnal Death Syndrome." *Macmillan Encyclopedia of Death and Dying*. Encyclopedia.com. Accessed May 28, 2024. www.encyclopedia.com/social-sciences/encyclopedias-almanacs-transcripts-and-maps/sudden-unexpected-nocturnal-death-syndrome.

Keenleyside, Anne, Margaret Bertulli, and Henry C. Fricke. "The Final Days of the Franklin Expedition: New Skeletal Evidence." *Arctic* 50, no. 1 (1997): 36–46. www.jstor.org/stable/40512040.

Lee, Diane. "Friday Night Frights: The Legend of Hawai'i's Night Marchers." *Honolulu Magazine*. Updated September 6, 2018. www.honolulumagazine.com/friday-night-frights-the-legend-of-hawaiis-night-marchers.

Logan, Diana. "Nurse Claims She Saw the Grim Reaper Take One of Her Patients." Exemplore. Published December 14, 2023. discover.hubpages.com/religion-philosophy/grim-reaper-visit-hospital.

Mgidi, Emily. "Tokoloshe 'Haunts' Families!," *Daily Sun*. Published March 18, 2021. thepaper.co.za/2021/03/18/tokoloshe-haunts-families.

Nelson, Sara C. "Ghost of 'La Llorona' Filmed at Crossing in Mexico City," *HuffPost UK*. Published September 23, 2016. www.huffingtonpost.co.uk/entry/ghost-of-la-llorona-filmed-at-crossing-in-mexico-city_uk_57e5077fe4b004d4d8629354.

New Straits Times. "Viral Video of 'Pontianak' Sighting—Hoax or Horror?" Published August 3, 2023. www.nst.com.my/news/nst-viral/2023/08/938429/nstviral-viral-video-pontianak-sighting-hoax-or-horror-watch.

Patagonia SouthernLand Expeditions. "The Magical Valley of Salamanca." Published April 30, 2019. patagoniasouthernlandexpeditions.com/2019/04/30/the-magical-valley-of-salamanca.

Puckett-Pope, Lauren. "'Unsolved Mysteries' Only Scratches the Surface of Japan's Eerie Post-Tsunami Ghost Sightings." *Cosmopolitan*. Published October 19, 2020. www.cosmopolitan.com/entertainment/tv/a34398241/japan-tsunami-ghost-sightings-true-story-unsolved-mysteries.

Stein, Ginny. "Mythical Mermaids Big Business in Zimbabwe." ABC (Australian Broadcasting Corporation) News. Updated April 29, 2012. www.abc.net.au/news/2012-04-29/mermaids-feared-in-landlocked-zimbabwe/3978462.

Stewart, Danny B. "Strange Sightings in Utah County: Don't Walk Alone After Dark." *Utah Stories*. Published October 26, 2021. utahstories.com/2021/10/strange-sightings-in-utah-county-dont-walk-alone-after-dark.

Index

Acknowledgments

To the cast of characters in my life's story, this book owes its heartbeat to you.

Tobie, my son and the second voice of *The Whispering Woods* podcast. May you always find the courage to face the unknown and the confidence to know that within you lies the power to conquer any challenge. And keep kicking monster butt.

Willow, my wonderful granddaughter, may your world be filled with wonder and your exclamations always be of awe and excitement. "Silly nanny" is just another way of saying "I love you." I know that!

Maisey, my daughter. Your voice is a melody that resonates with the uniqueness of who you are. Never be afraid to sing your truth, loud and proud.

George, my son. You have a courageous spirit, but may you keep both feet firmly on the ground as, no, you cannot fly so please don't try again, ever.

Roger, my partner, thank you for being the calm in every storm and the companion on every journey, no matter how mundane or magical.

Molly, for sharing the simple joys of watching slasher movies. Your ability to not cover your eyes is a real superpower.

Mum and Bob, your unwavering support and faith have meant everything on my darkest days.

❧ ACKNOWLEDGMENTS ❧

Becky and Rachael, because sisters are the co-authors of our childhood stories and, as they say, the cheerleaders in our adult triumphs, and you get a mention because, well, "I wrote a book!!!"

Dad for giving me the love of all things spooky and supernatural.

To Tyler, Jacob, Kelvin, Beth, Emma, Sinead, John, Ava, Luca, and Leo, who make my motley crew complete.

Natalie, my oldest friend, for letting me share one of her many stories and to Matt, my work wife, and his wife Janie.

In loving memory of Vic and Eira, whose stories continue in the legacy they've left behind.

Elizabeth for baby-stepping me through the process and dealing with my imposter syndrome, Rage for giving me the opportunity, and everyone else at Quarto for turning my ramblings into a book.

And to you, dear reader, for joining me on this journey. May your days be filled with joy and your nights be filled with monsters.

I wrote a book!!! And you all played your part in its creation. Thank you.

About the Author

Sarah J H Powell is a co-host of *The Whispering Woods* podcast, a show that delves into the dark and mysterious world of folklore, supernatural, and the unexplained. She has been fascinated by the paranormal since she was a child and was given a book by her late grandfather about haunted objects. She would also listen to her mother read the original, often gruesomely macabre, fairy tales by the Brothers Grimm and lapped up every moment. Sarah is a mother of three and a grandmother of one. She lives in Bristol, England, with her two youngest children where she enjoys reading and crafts, as well as going on hikes with her partner to spooky and strange places.

Sarah hosts the podcast with her son Tobie, who inherited his mother's love for the spooky and the strange. Together, they share their own experiences and research on various topics, from urban legends to ancient myths. You can listen to *The Whispering Woods* podcast at www.thewhisperingwoodspodcast.com or follow them on Instagram @thewhisperingwoodspodcast.

First published in 2025 by Wellfleet Press,
an imprint of The Quarto Group,
142 West 36th Street, 4th Floor,
New York, NY 10018, USA
(212) 779-4972
www.Quarto.com

Wellfleet titles are also available at discount for retail, wholesale, promotional, and bulk purchase.
For details, contact the Special Sales Manager by email at specialsales@quarto.com or by mail at The
Quarto Group, Attn: Special Sales Manager, 100 Cummings Center Suite 265D, Beverly, MA 01915 USA.

10 9 8 7 6 5 4 3 2 1

ISBN: 978-1-57715-439-6

Digital edition published in 2025
eISBN: 978-0-7603-8988-1

Library of Congress Cataloging-in-Publication Data

Names: Powell, Sarah J. H., author.
Title: Tales from the whispering woods : stories of fear and folklore from
  the dark forest / Sarah J H Powell.
Description: New York, NY : Castle, 2025. | Includes bibliographical
  references and index. | Summary: "Tales from the Whispering Woods draws
  out the similarities among iconic figures of creepy folklore,
  superstitions, and urban legends while at the same time highlighting
  their unique cultural characteristics, all brought to you by the host of
  the Whispering Woods podcast"-- Provided by publisher.
Identifiers: LCCN 2024035418 (print) | LCCN 2024035419 (ebook) | ISBN
  9781577154396 (hardcover) | ISBN 9780760389881 (ebook)
Subjects: LCSH: Folklore. | Superstition. | Urban folklore. | Horror tales.
  | Podcasting.
Classification: LCC GR81 .P68 2025 (print) | LCC GR81 (ebook) | DDC
  398.2--dc23/eng/20241104
LC record available at https://lccn.loc.gov/2024035418
LC ebook record available at https://lccn.loc.gov/2024035419

Group Publisher: Rage Kindelsperger
Editorial Director: Erin Canning
Creative Director: Laura Drew
Managing Editor: Cara Donaldson
Editor: Elizabeth You
Cover Design: Scott Richardson
Interior Design: Annie Marino

Printed in China